A Shouting in the Desert

Jesus' Kind of Kingdom

J.P. Allen

Broadman Press/Nashville, Tennessee

© Copyright 1976 • Broadman Press
All rights reserved

4281-28
ISBN: 0-8054-8128-1

Dewey Decimal Classification: 232.95
Subject heading: JESUS CHRIST—TEACHINGS

Library of Congress Catalog Card Number: 76-2239
Printed in the United States of America

To

Dottie

lover, partner, and friend
this book is affectionately
dedicated

Preface

There is an urgency about the kingdom of heaven that needs a shouting cry in the spiritual deserts of the late twentieth century. In an era when an excess of religious teachers of every stripe have surfaced to establish their own dominions, it is my conviction that the characteristics of Christ's kingdom ought to have re-statement from Jesus' view. It is *his* kingdom, by his purchase and lordship, and only he has the right to state its terms.

Too much spongy thinking has defined the King of kings as though he were a personal possession: Individuals speak glibly about "having Jesus." Spiritual hucksters peddle comfort and ease in his name: "Try Jesus." There are dangers inherent in the contemporary vocabulary of piety: one is an easy familiarity with spiritual things which causes people to cry "Lord, Lord," but not to do the things which he says. And there is always the temptation to try to "use" Jesus on one's own conditions: He saves our souls and we have sweet fellowship with him, but our employment in his realm is our option. Quite as perilous is the deadly toll of mere tradition, the repetition of cliché and custom, until our tenets, tightly held, come to bear little resemblance to New Testament doctrine. It is like children copying their own mistakes in a copybook; unless there is constant regard for the original model, any error is sure to be compounded.

Of course it is given to every Christian to interpret what the Master said, and we do not need to agree. This does not trouble me. I am fearful, rather, of the growing numbers of religious leaders who have not concerned themselves with Jesus' own defi-

nitions. Those have too often obscured and distorted the intent
of the Lord. There are people telling us what Jesus wants of
us who have never studied his declarations as to the boundaries
and conditions of Kingdom citizenship. Everyone who speaks in
his name must examine his commission or risk the fearful judgment
which falls on the false prophet.

I heard the preaching of the outstanding Methodist missionary,
E. Stanley Jones, at a formative period in my ministry. I still
recall his zeal in responding to a critic: "It is said by some that
I am obsessed with the kingdom of God. That is true, and it
is a *magnificent obsession.*" It was the era when the book of
that title was popular. Something of his ardor, strongly reinforced
by the New Testament interpretations of W. H. Davis, kindled
a spark in me. In Jesus' instructions regarding that kingdom I
find both the warmest relationship to Jesus the friend and the
binding claim on my life of Christ the King. But above all, it
is a true kingdom—he is the king, and we are his stewards,
responsible and chargeable. We shall all err, but let no one contest
with Jesus Christ his sovereign rights, even in ignorance.

John the Baptist put it right—prepare the way *of the Lord;*
make *his* paths straight—his, not ours!

All scriptural references are to the Revised Standard Version,
except as otherwise noted.

                                                J. P. ALLEN

Fort Worth, Texas

Contents

I
A Shouting in the Desert
Jesus' Kind of Kingdom

"Hark! Someone is shouting in the desert,
'Get the Lord's way ready,
Make his paths straight.'"
(Mark 1:3, Goodspeed)

The desert is a foreboding place. The searing sun rules the day and yields only to the bone-deep chill of night. The undulating terrain is punctuated with stark silhouettes carved by relentless winds. Its scrub growth seems insufficient to support man's life, and shifting sands defy his habitation. It is hostile; man fears it. The desolation and silence overawe him.

Logically, then, the desert has always provided a natural setting for drama. The eerie stillness lends an air of mystery, and whatever is there is different, fearful. The heat creates disturbing illusions which tantalize the mind. The desert's magnitude intimidates even the venturesome, for it is beyond his range of normal. Death seems to lurk there within the unexpected.

Since the Bible is the drama of God's redemptive purpose, it is no wonder that so many scriptural events took place against a desert backdrop.[1] To the writing prophets one particular area loomed especially large—the burning wastes which stretched from the city of Jerusalem to the waters of Babylon, the great Syrian Desert. It represented to them an immeasurable space, the distance between the glory that was once Zion's and the unbearable humiliation of captivity.

Isaiah, seven centuries before Christ, had foretold Judah's peril; but his warning went unheeded. He had lived and preached amid earthshaking events. His was the era of Assyria's ascendency, the

---

[1] Note among others Abraham's trek from Ur, the exodus wanderings, Elijah's flight, the magi, the temptation of Jesus, and Paul's three years of solitude in Arabia. The words *desert* or *wilderness* appear 334 times in the Scriptures (RSV).

11

rise of Sargon and Sennacherib, the fall of Samaria and the ten
northern tribes of Israel. He predicted Babylon's world dominion
a hundred years in advance of its coming and daringly told his
monarch, Hezekiah, the vivid details (Isa. 39:5-7).

The following century and a half vindicated the seer. Neither
king nor commoner repented at the call of Jehovah's messengers;
and, like Samaria, proud Jerusalem was destroyed, the people
enslaved by Nebuchadnezzar in 587 B.C. But the weary years in
exile had achieved their purpose—and now, at long last, the
prophetic voice is raised again. This time the note of comfort,
hope, restoration is dominant. Now for the captive nation the
prophet of God foresees the prospects of home. God intended
to intervene in history. He had purposes which included even
the haughty monarchs of Babylon and Persia, and the time of
their fulfillment draws near. It is to such a moment that Isaiah's
poems of chapter 40 are addressed.

It is as though a skilled theatrical director is producing the
drama. The stage setting is the desert. A hush of expectancy is
in the air. The scene is set for a significant moment in history
which must be played out on a grandiose scale, and a supremely
important proclamation is about to be made. The imperious voice
of a herald reverberates across the desert from a mountain height,
"Cry . . . . Proclaim!" No less a setting is adequate for the
portrayal of the sovereign God advancing to his kingdom.

> "A *voice cries:*
> '*In the wilderness prepare the way of the Lord,*
> *make straight in the desert a highway for our*
> *God*'" (*Isa. 40:3*).

The voice is not identified, but the speaker is the celestial agent
of the Almighty. History is not without evidences that both kings
and conquerors had valleys filled and obstacles removed which

might impede their victorious march. So God, immanent in the affairs of men, declared that even the desert must be no hindrance to the route he was determined to follow. Nor did the course of empire deter him. Cyrus the Great, king of Persia, would have been shocked if he could have read Isaiah 45:1-8, in which he himself was named as one of the Lord's anointed servants. He could only have been incredulous that the God of the Israelites who were his bond servants was in control of history!

ANOTHER DESERT—ANOTHER VOICE

But now it is another time, another voice. The chosen people did return home to Jerusalem, purified for Jehovah's use. Babylon and Persia fell; Alexander and the Greeks had come and gone. The Macabbees secured independence for the Jews for a hundred years. Then came the Romans—and the clock was winding down toward the zero hour of history, the birth of Jesus Christ!

John Mark was not insensitive to the pageantry which accompanied the Messiah's advent, so the first word of the gospel sounded a note of high drama. Mark is generally agreed to have first written of the good news of Jesus Christ (Mark 1:1). One can almost see him searching for his opening lines. How should he clothe with language the climactic fact of all history? With what words could he do justice to the most elevated theme ever spoken or penned? What if his imagination were too small to be the human instrument of the God of the creation and of redemption?

The mind of the Gospel writer turned back to a parallel in Israel's history so prophetic that it was fitting to introduce the world's greatest news. Isaiah's picture of the messenger crying in the desert for the preparation of the way of the Lord seemed to Mark to have found fulfillment. It had happened. A strange figure of a man had stridden out of the Judean wastes and had created a sensation in the land. Mark recorded it in stark simplicity: "John the baptizer appeared in the wilderness" (Mark 1:4).

Once again Jehovah was about to act in the drama of revelation, and again the desert was the stage. But this time the spotlight turned full on the herald who announced the prologue. In Isaiah the "voice" was unidentified; now he is portrayed in vivid detail. His was a strange manner and a different role, but John the Forerunner knew his call. He was not God's message; he was only the messenger. At the height of the excitement he created in Judea, he was ordered by a committee of the priestly officials from Jerusalem to identify himself. "Who are you? . . . What do you say about yourself?" His answer was unequivocal: "I am the voice of one crying in the wilderness, 'Make straight the way of the Lord,' as the prophet Isaiah said" (John 1:22,23).

The first duty of the emissary of a king is to get an audience, and the baptizer was apt for that. He came to excite and alarm, to shake men from spiritual lethargy, and to heighten expectancy. His appearance, his clothing, and his message accomplished such a purpose. He was a man of mystery and was cast in the mold of the rugged prophets of those storied years when God spoke to his people through bold preachers like Elijah and Amos. In the eyes of the people in the regions of Jerusalem, John the Baptist was "a real prophet" (Mark 11:32).

This alone was sufficient reason for the instant popularity of this man of the desert. The prophetic voice had been muted too long. Evidence of this dearth is seen in a saying of the people in reaction to Jesus' miraculous raising of the son of a widow from the village of Nain. A sense of fear seized them in the presence of his divine power, and they remarked, "A great prophet has arisen among us!" and "God has visited his people!" (Luke 7:16). It had, indeed, been a long time since Ezra and Malachi.

There are evidences that the prolonged silence of God in the interbiblical period [2] had produced a mood of readiness in the Jewish nation. Indeed, it is alleged that a spirit of expectancy prevailed in the Graeco-Roman world. Seutonius, a Roman biogra-

---

[2] In round figures, some four hundred years between the close of the Old Testament and the opening of the New.

pher who lived from A.D. 69 until after 122, declared, "There had spread over all the orient an old and established belief, that it was fated at that time for men coming from Judea to rule the world." Tacitus, a historian of the same period, said, "There was a firm persuasion that at this very time the East was to grow powerful, and that rulers coming from Judea were to acquire universal empire." Thus would Romans react to anticipation of the advent of an illustrious figure. Josephus, himself a Jew, translated the sense of readiness in Israel as a general belief that "about that time one from their country should become governor of the habitable earth." The best evidence comes from the Scriptures. Luke the historian put it simply, "As the people were in expectation . . . ." (Luke 3:15).

THE KING IS COMING

Against such a backdrop John, the uncouth preacher from nowhere, was nothing less than a sensation. He was instantly the subject of speculation in the marketplace. The common man saw in him a champion, and masses flocked to his cause. The rough cloak of skin set him dramatically apart from the dull and deadening teachers in Jerusalem. The excitement of his message promised something more than endless conformity to tedious scribal traditions and regulations. John's declaration that a superlative person and event were about to arrive persuaded the people to confess their sins and be identified with the new order.

But the doings in the desert reached also into the precincts of priestly power and created quite another mood. The thunder they heard from the Jordan shook the establishment. If this were to be another religious fad that periodically flared, well and good. On the other hand, it began to appear to the Jewish authorities that a threat existed which could not be ignored. The baptizer's preaching had a permanent ring to it. Someone was staking out a kingdom, and foundations were being poured.

As long as John presumed to be only a teacher and reformer,

the powerful ruling religious parties had no cause to fear the unlettered and unauthorized seer. They could handle him as they had others. But they did not miss the significance of his dominant note, "Someone is coming." Perhaps one statement he made disturbed them most deeply. The coming one, the Forerunner taunted them, was not remote but was *at hand:* "Among you stands one whom you do not know" (John 1:26). To men already paranoid about their power that was a crowning blow.

The fear of the Pharisees and Sadducees was well founded. They read John correctly. God was not only going to speak; he was about to arrive! "The way of the Lord" which had for so long been prophetic was suddenly to become a contemporary event. No longer would king or priest or prophet represent Jehovah. He, himself, was now to enter history and set up his reign—a new kingdom with a new kind of man! This is what John the Baptist was shouting about.

So "the gospel" was the startling news that the King had come and had established his kingdom. The dominant theme of Jesus' teaching was the kingdom of heaven. It was fitting, then, for the Forerunner to speak in terms of sovereignty and might. Each of the four Gospel narratives paints a portrait of the Master in unique form and feature, yet it is always the same Jesus. One universal characteristic is never far from the surface in the New Testament record: It is that the Messiah-King is always presented in colors of royalty. Why not? A kingdom has its sovereign, and Jesus Christ rules in the unique realm he came to establish. He was a servant, true, but a Servant-King. He is certainly a Savior; but he is also Lord of all creation. He is a friend, as his followers have discovered; but to be his friend is to be a friend of the omnipotent God.

The four Gospel narratives attest to his kingliness. His lineage was traced to David's royal line. The time and place of his birth were ascertained by Herod the king for the magi who came looking for a king. Gifts fit for majesty were presented in his childhood.

Satan was astute enough to cloak his temptation in a stratagem which might appeal a ruler; he offered Jesus "the kingdoms of the world." Jesus presented the constitution and bylaws of his realm in the Sermon on the Mount—the manifesto of the King. His miracles were his royal credentials. Throughout his ministry he never lost his calm and regal bearing. Through the parables he revealed the mysteries of his regime to those who accepted his sway. He triumphantly entered the capital city to the acclaim of thousands. In the hours of his sufferings he affirmed his supremacy over legions of angels should he will to summon them. He went to his cross with the taunting inscription over his head declaring that he was "the King of the Jews." Meant to be mockery, the words were, as was often the case, more prophetic than they knew. He was sovereign in death, and the earth shook at the last breath of its Creator. All-conquering in his resurrection, his last words were that of a potentate: "All authority in heaven and on earth has been given to me." The parables of his return at the end of the age are couched in the language of preeminence. He pictured himself as a Lord receiving an accounting from his stewards and as a king sitting on a judgment throne.

Tacitus, then, as already quoted, was not unrealistic in anticipating a ruler from Judea who was "to acquire universal empire." Christendom needs again, as it repeatedly has, to discover that it is subject to an overlord, one of paramount rank. The humble manger does not obscure his royalty or dominion. It is too easy at Easter to stand and shout with Handel "King of Kings and Lord of Lords," but when religion is "out of season" to relegate Jesus to the posture of a plaintive outsider knocking at doors whose rooms are terribly preoccupied. Jesus Christ has never surrendered his scepter; he is not an intruder, an interloper, or an alternative to be ignored or turned down.

Man does not have an option on the crown-rights of the Savior. He does have choice, but not as to whether there shall be consequences. The option is whether to be a son of the kingdom or a rebel in the hands of a supreme monarch. This is his domain. He rules it with compassion and graciousness, but he will judge his creatures with exacting righteousness. The whole creation looks toward the day when "at the name of Jesus every knee should bow, in heaven and on earth and under the earth, and every tongue confess that Jesus Christ is Lord, to the glory of God the Father" (Phil. 2:10).

HIS KIND OF KINGDOM

The Forerunner's burden, however, was not solely to proclaim the advent of the King. It was his as well to mark clearly the boundaries of the realm so that people would know what kind of kingdom it was to be. Not to comprehend the nature of the King's reign would negate any responsible commitment to follow him, then or now.

John's contemporaries needed such definition. They considered Israel to be even then the dominion of Jehovah; they already belonged. So fixed was this notion that at the close of Jesus' earthly ministry his most devoted followers asked of him, "Lord, will you at this time restore the kingdom to Israel?" (Acts 1:6). They were looking for a return to the ancient civil polity and a theocratic rule. The message of the baptizer and Jesus was that a totally new concept was being instituted. God's people would no longer be his by birthright but by a spiritual rebirth. It was to be a "heavenly" regime with a citizenship of a higher order, not a new edition of an old kingdom. A new contract (covenant) was about to be drawn, and the terms would be radically different from the old. The preaching of the herald and the Messiah made that abundantly clear.

John initiated the contrast by suggesting fire as being of higher order than water and thereby a sign of the rule of Christ—"I baptize you with water; but he who is mightier than I is coming . . . he will baptize you with the Holy Spirit and with fire" (Luke 3:16; see also Mark 1:8). As would any preacher, John the Baptist listened for the reactions to his proclamation. The first he encountered was the claim that the old was good enough. The people were content! He knew the murmuring in the multitude, possibly prompted by the Pharisees and Sadducees. He boldly, therefore, confronted their claims to have no need for admission to the new kingdom because, they said, "We have Abraham as our father" (Luke 3:8; Matt. 3:9). John declared that excuse invalid. "Do not make it as a proposition to yourselves," he cried—that is the force of the language he used. Looking for an analogy of utter futility, his eyes perhaps chanced upon the loose stones lying on the banks of the Jordan. Then he challenged their vaunted heritage by claiming that God could easily make other sons of Abraham from the rocks should he please and was therefore not dependent on them for the continuation of father Abraham's posterity. Indeed, they were expendable; they could be readily set aside in the purposes of God if they refused to hear the requirements for sonship to God.

Some of them heard and were moved to act. Already belonging to the commonwealth of Israel, they asked John, "What then shall we do?" (Luke 3:10). His answer unmistakably demanded evidences of a drastic change within—new attitudes, new hearts, new deeds. In short, new men for a new kind of kingdom! The old would never again suffice.

The stage setting on which the first chapters of the New Testament were played out is rich in symbolism. The prophetic voice of the new era arose from the bleak dryland wastes and promised a new day. Light streamed from the desert against four centuries of spiritual darkness; "the light" had come. The barrenness of scribal and traditional religion was set in sharp contrast to the vibrant message of repentance and its fruit. Jesus completed the picture of vitality and refreshment by claiming that whoever drank from him "the water that I shall give him will become in him a spring of water welling up to eternal life" (John 4:14).

John the Baptist served his purpose and introduced Jesus to

center stage. From the moment of the Master's first words all
the people knew they were hearing strange doctrines. Officers
sent to arrest him expressed it pointedly: "No man ever spoke
like this man!" (John 7:46). The novelty of his teachings was readily
accepted by common men as the fresh breath of life, but to the
religious establishment it had the sound of rank heresy. They
accused him of destroying the foundations of the law and the
prophets on which Israel existed.

Jesus would not let such an attack go unchallenged. He categor-
ically denied that he had come to revoke God's law or to nullify
his promises. God had not changed his mind. To the contrary,
he had been working through the ages to arrive at such a moment.
At this juncture, the great Teacher introduced a pivotal idea—fulfillment!

"To fulfill" is to bring a thing to its intended end, to accomplish
a design. A flower is the fulfillment of a planted seed and the
cultivated bud. The man is the fulfillment of the promise in the
baby boy. The terms and conditions of Jehovah's covenant with
Abraham and his law given through Moses had never been given
permanent status. Always there was the futuristic look: the Messiah
would appear; the "day of the Lord" would arrive in his own
time. Favorite phrases of the prophets were "in those days" and
"it shall come to pass." Jeremiah constructed a graphic figure
of speech which perfectly depicted the purpose of God when
it was time to work it out in history. Every Hebrew knew of
the stone tablets on which Moses brought God's laws to the
wilderness wanderers. Against that knowledge, the prophet wrote,
"But this is the covenant which I will make with the house of
Israel after those days, says the Lord: I will put my law within
them, and I will write it upon their hearts; and I will be their
God, and they shall be my people" (Jer. 31:33).

What would be the characteristics of a religion whose tenets
were inscribed in human hearts? What superiority to have the
disciplines of faith exercised from within rather than imposed by

regulation and prohibition! Christ gave himself for *that kind* of kingdom. In his scheme commandment gives way to conversion; precept is replaced by relationship; belief is not creedal but creative. His disciples are not bond servants to law; they are sons. For the children of the kingdom discipline is not taking a beating, but graduating from kindergarten. In regard to legalism, they know not manacles but emancipation. No longer are they hemmed in by restraining bars without—these have been replaced by structural steel within. The motive is no longer "thou shalt" but "I will."

Such a radical departure from all previous religious norms is at the core of the uniqueness of the Christian faith. It has become the cornerstone of the kingdom of heaven, and every citizen is a vital part of that creative relationship. No one has a vote on what kind of realm it was designed to be, and the issues on which Jesus spoke clearly are never up for a referendum. All evangelism must measure itself against his standards. No invitation to bear the name of Jesus Christ is valid unless it enunciates every condition he put forth. Each of his churches always operates under his banner; and he is the present, indwelling Sovereign. Whoever cheaply wears the name of Jesus, whoever shapes the Master's doctrines to his own ends, whoever proclaims the Lord's name out of ulterior motive does so to his own peril. It is no small matter to contest with him who declared "I will build my church" and then called it his bride. The King will not yield on the nature of his kingdom!

The innovation by Jesus of an entirely new concept of religious community was the only hope of saving worship and life from the deadening results of all prior systems. No teacher, priest, or prophet had ever dreamed of propositions or rites except those which could be satisfied by obedience and performance. The devotee did what was commanded and largely dismissed the obligations until they were next due. But whatever was done would be repeated, and on a prescribed schedule. The holy day would return; the sacrifice would be rescheduled, the place and manner stipulated, the priest appointed. Thus it had always been, and thus it was expected to be. Man would forever be a slave to the system.

Jesus abruptly broke the vicious cycle. His was a daring revelation, and it brought down the wrath of the vested interests and the unimaginative upon his head. But it spared Christianity in its essence from two inevitable effects of the old religious institutions.

Traditional religion.—There is no impropriety in tradition per se, obviously. The danger comes at the point of blindly accepting the tradition rather than the truth or fact which originally produced the tradition. Jesus went to the heart of the issue in Matthew 5 with his repeated "You have heard that it was said . . . ." That was the problem; it was said, and said, and said—dinned into the mind until the critical faculty was dulled. Concepts were accepted blindly, unexplored and unreasoned. That kind of performance cuts the heart out of religion, and the routine practices lose meaning because they have lost relevance to any real situation. The men of an American service club assembled in weekly session and opened the meeting with the customary pledge to the flag. Hands over hearts, they faced the podium and solemnly intoned, "I pledge allegiance to the flag . . . ." The pledge completed, the members sat down to lunch; and only two or three noticed that the salute had been given to the Canadian flag which had been inadvertently moved to the wrong side of the platform. It was a tradition to offer the pledge, an accepted thing to do, but what should have had meaning became a mockery.

A prime motive of the Master was to produce a fellowship so alive and creative that rote tradition could not emerge. Thus the commandments of Jesus did not lend themselves so much to obedience as to individual investigation. He affirmed that life does not consist of the abundance of a man's possessions, but he left it to a lifetime quest to determine the things of which it *does* consist. He commanded his devotees to seek his kingdom as a first affection, but he gave no specifics as to what comprised that priority or how to achieve it. He invited his disciples to follow him, but only hinted at how far or along what paths they should keep company with him. It was not that such details could not be known; it was, rather, that they must not be laid down as a uniform directive in advance. They could, however, be determined progressively. Believers would not be following him by regulations described or conditions prescribed. Instead, he would guide them personally. He would be with them as they walked in the way. Why should he leave directions as though he were going away? He was not going to leave them!

His use of parables as a major tool of teaching played a significant role in producing his kingdom style. The parable yields its truth only to those who have eyes to see and ears to hear the word-pictures which came often to his lips. In any age, and to the believer in whatever stage of spiritual development, the parable is a promise of hidden treasure. But the disciple must care about his Lord and what he said, or there is no reason to investigate. When one does unearth a pearl of great price, it is not a chant or a dogma or an article of faith.

It is not that the kingdom man is not under orders; the issue is the *kind* of authority to which he gives allegiance. As with husband and wife, there are rules. But the regulations are not imposed from without; nor are they uniformly applied to every individual alike. They did not merely derive from tradition. There are rules in marriage, but the rules come out of the relationship! That is the way Christ is related to those who bear his name.

Formal religion.—The issue bears no relationship to orderliness in church polity and practice or to structured services of worship. These are right and good and subject to individual preference and need. The peril is at the point of the human tendency to substitute form for fact and to worship the form.

The alert is sounded in Christianity in the instance of any

teaching or exhortation which can be accomplished by *doing* it
and then setting it aside. To do one's duty as though the act
discharges the obligation is to return to worn and discarded systems
of religion. For some such reason, at least in part, Jesus appeared
to renounce "fractions" in the economy of his kingdom. Two
fractions had been elevated by the priests and scribes of his day
to such preeminence that they had almost obscured the reason
for the divine commands.

One-seventh was the paramount fraction, the one that brought
Jesus' first clashes with the Pharisees and rulers. The sabbath rest
was one of God's basic commandments. Jesus himself observed
it. Yet the elaborate embroidery of hundreds of years of scribal
commentary had distorted God's intent and brought men into
bondage to empty forms.[3] Jesus reprimanded those who burdened
the people with regulations not of God's authority. He reversed
their emphasis. "The sabbath," he said, "was made for man, not
man for the sabbath" (Mark 2:27). Under Jesus' sovereignty his
people did not belong to God one-seventh of the time. They should
observe a day holy to the Lord, but his stress was that *all* of
a man's life was the Lord's. No one "buys off" the Almighty with
a seventh part of his time. Kingdom citizens are always his.

One-tenth also caused people to stumble. God instituted the
tithe, and Jesus raised it to a level more binding than any legal
enactment. But to act as though the Master has claim on only
one-tenth of one's possessions reduces tithing to a type of bribe.
Pay God his part and do with the rest as you will! A tenth, in
that way of thinking, is God's and the larger fraction is none
of his affair! Under the new covenant the stewardship of *all* of
life is the theme. The tithe is a token of the totality of divine
ownership. How one earns and spends the nine-tenths is a legitimate part of his accountability.

---

[3] Some scholars spent a lifetime debating single issues on sabbath observance.
Entire volumes were written on how far one could travel on the seventh day
or how much could be lifted without its being called work.

It was a distinctive of the new realm that for the first time a question forever asked was no longer valid. *"How much* do I have to do . . . give . . . spend?" The issue of "is not that enough?" was settled once for all. No man can purchase, by deed or gift, an exemption or discharge. The disciple of Christ is in kingdom partnership with his Lord. To any such questions the answer will always be "You shall love the Lord your God with all your heart, and with all your soul, and with all your mind, and with all your strength" (Mark 12:30). The Christian never arrives; he is always on his way!

OTHER TIMES—OTHER DESERTS

It may be profitable to reach back to Isaiah and Mark once more and borrow their symbolism. Periodically there have been eras of spiritual drought. The desert seems to encroach on the vitality of religion. The wells run dry, and this lament is often appropriate: "How tedious and tasteless the hour when Jesus no longer I see."

One condition nearly always contributes to periods of dryness in faith—when life is overwhelmingly complex. When severe issues fracture societal harmony and when economic stress and political strife distract people from the more creative joys of living, then people are pessimistic and preoccupied. The dry winds brown the spiritual landscape.

The last third of the twentieth century bears all these earmarks. Accompanying them is the lure to oversimplification, refuge in rules, living by rote, comfort in commandments. It is too painful to live with all the question marks, too difficult to think through the issues; so the public readily accepts pat definitions and dogmatic answers. It is simpler to follow tradition than to blaze new trails; easier to obey commandments than to apply principles; less complicated to submit to external authority than to practice internal disciplines.

The church does not exist in insulation or in ball-bearing suspension. It cannot escape the environment, but it does not need to accommodate to it either. In such a time the kingdom requires maturing sons and daughters who seize and straighten out question marks, dare to cross new frontiers, and major on relationships rather than regulations. Creative discipleship is the call of the King. Of paramount importance, then, is that every Christian comprehend the *terms of discipleship!* What kind of kingdom is the kingdom of heaven?

The time is ripe for fearless and imaginative prophets to add a new note of excitement to the "way of the Lord." His heralds must stride from the barren wilderness, wherever it may exist, and "make his paths straight."

Let there be heard a shouting in the desert again!

II
When Time Was Ripe

The Advent of the King

"And this is in harmony with God's merciful purpose for the government of the world when the times are ripe for it."
(Eph. 1:10, Weymouth)[1]

It is likely that the nativity scene of contemporary Christmas pageantry bears little resemblance to the crude shelter where the Christ was born. The modern version is compounded of medieval idealization and the artistic imagination of theatrical directors. In actuality the manger was a trough or crib in a stall, perhaps hewn from the native limestone, and possibly even located in a cave.

Travel accommodations in the Middle East were few and primitive. Families on the move were usually self-contained, packing their own shelter, food, and supplies. The "inns," such as they were, generally comprised a lodging-house, often opening onto a courtyard. Around the court might be a range of arches or an open gallery, beyond which were the stalls where donkeys, camels, or goats were sheltered. "Manger" literally means a place where animals feed. On such a bed Mary laid the newborn King.

She wore no robe of royal blue; no light shimmered above her head; no music echoed around the scene; and there were no angels there. But they were not sharing the quarters with the cattle or livestock. These had been moved, and the place had been cleaned by the host and made fit for human habitation. The only "music" was the sounds of ordinary living. The light was from open oil lamps supplementing whatever sunlight entered through the door of the stall. The woman was young, possibly no more than eighteen or nineteen, of strong peasant stock and

---

[1] From *Weymouth's New Testament in Modern Speech*, Richard Francis Weymouth, Harper and Row, Publishers.

clothed like all the other women of the village. It is probable that she had never heard the sound of the word *Mary* or the Grecized form *Maria*. They called her Miriam.

THE MEN AT THE MANGER

The major discrepancy between fact and fiction, however, may well be the cast of characters. As always depicted, the shepherds were there—although they may have been no more than two or three. Yet, contrary to most pageants, the magi were not there! They arrived from one to two years later, when Mary and Joseph lived with the child in a house (Matt. 2:11)—and they may have been many more than three. But to those with an eye for imagination and a sensitivity to God's timing, there were others present on that eventful day. Three shadowy figures can be discerned in the background. Each one of them played a vital role in God's plan for the ages, and each was an instrument in history to bring to fruition his "merciful purpose for the government of the world when the times are ripe."

It is obvious that Abraham would have to be there when the promise was fulfilled. The mainstream of God's redemptive plan began with him. Called out from polytheism, in the loneliness of his wanderings he came to know the one true God. He became an intimate of the Almighty; and to Abraham, more perhaps than to any other, God disclosed the promises which established the unique covenant with Israel.[2] From that time the direction of the Hebrew nation was determined.

Abraham, therefore, represents in the nativity picture a spiritual preparation, the unique Jewish contribution to religious thought—an ethical monotheism. The Son of God could have never been manifested had there remained the risk that Jesus would be thought to be just another deity. The centuries of bitter discipline had caused Israel to put away all idols and false gods.

---

[2] Among several conversations between Abraham and God, the one recorded in Genesis 17:1-8 best sets forth the covenant relationship.

They were at last convinced that Jehovah was the one God, and they served him alone. Against such a faith, even though it was a stumbling block to Jesus' contemporaries, God could reveal himself as Father and as Son. It was through Abraham and his seed that Jehovah manifested who he was and what he intended to do. The ancient patriarch, looking on the infant Messiah, would have been completely fulfilled.

By the side of father Abraham one sees a handsome young Greek. Endowed with beauty and genius, Alexander the Great at thirty-one had conquered his world—from Macedonia to India. At thirty-three he died in Babylon. He had been more than a brilliant commander; he had introduced into the East the first concept of the worth of the individual. As he gave significance to the common man he gave him also a universal tongue—the Greek language. It is said that upon an occasion Aristotle, tutor of the boy Alexander, had warned him to remember the difference between Greek and barbarian. Alexander answered, "I will make the whole world Greek."

It was this accomplishment that thrust Alexander into God's time schedule. He had no other right to involvement, even symbolically, with the kind of kingdom Jesus founded. He fashioned a worldwide communications system along which the gospel of Jesus Christ was broadcast. Hitherto, Europe and Asia had been split into tiny linguistic cells. Languages and dialects isolated men's minds and left them incapable of common experience or expression. How could the good news ever be told or a written revelation be possible until speech was understood? The plan for the world could henceforth be told to the world. The Macedonian belonged in the picture.

Caesar was there as well. What the Greek did for language the Roman did for government. The Mediterranean world was fragmented into innumerable states and nations. Petty rulers held sway over domains often no larger than a modern city. Fortified frontiers were a barrier to transients and would have been impassable to the missionaries of the infant church. Major transportation routes were unknown except in the case of a few far-flung empires—Persia, for example. Caravan trails, perilous mountain passes, and unmarked river fords served the infrequent travelers within the kingdoms; and the threats of capricious tax levies and marauding bandits were constant hazards. Significant interstate or international routes were yet-undreamed-of luxuries.

But the Caesars changed all that. Other conquerors had fashioned huge empires, but their conquests lacked permanence and the genius for colonization. Roman dominion prevailed on three continents and embraced the widest diversity of races and cultures. Yet by military might and efficient administration the city on the Tiber forged its empire into a workable unit and inaugurated a system of law that became the model for the Western world.

Tying the unwieldy jurisdiction together was a network of roads, some of which still stand after twenty centuries. The Latin word used by Julius Caesar was that he "fortified" a road. These arteries crisscrossed the realm and the traffic of troops; couriers and commerce flowed freely, always under the protection of the government. A Roman citizen could traverse the empire from Damascus to Spain with safety and without special travel documents. Along these highways marched Caesar's legions, and behind them trudged the advance guard of another powerful army—Paul, Silas, Timothy, Luke. From Syria to Gibraltar they went on Caesar's roads, but under Christ's banner.

Truly the time was ripe. Only when all the necessary conditions prevailed could the redemptive story be told. It was not enough for a purified Judaism to be ready to produce the essential characters. There was a world preparation required to accomplish God's purpose. He had not presided over history through the ages in order to make a provincial announcement. His kingdom was a universal dominion, and the advent of the Savior was "good news of a great joy which will come to all the people" (Luke 2:10). It was when Abraham and Alexander and Caesar could meet that the times were "in harmony with God's merciful purpose for the government of the world." God had waited for the climax of history, but no more. The fullness of time had come, and Jesus could be born!

A People Prepared

The flame of Jewish messianic expectancy burned low and occasionally flickered, but it never went out. A prime reason for the preservation of Israel's brave hopes is evident in the events God used to move the divine scheme onto the human stage. The priesthood had in many instances come into disrepute. Infected by the corruption of the high priestly office through its political ties, the priests were often empty functionaries, devoid of spiritual vitality, serving by rote the prescribed rituals. But not all. Some were devout and sensitive, both to their ministries and to the role of Israel as God's chosen nation. Such was Zechariah, father of the herald of the Messiah-King.

The overture to the royal birth narrative was spoken, appropriately, by a heavenly messenger come to earth with an announcement. Zechariah, the priest, lived with his wife, Elizabeth, in the hill country south of Jerusalem. His section of priests [3] was on duty in the Temple, and to him had fallen the lot of entering the holy place at the hour of prayer and burning incense upon the golden altar. It was the crowning moment of his priestly life. When sacrifice was made for the whole nation, a cloud of incense billowed from the altar as a fitting offering of praise and prayer to Jehovah. Outside, in the Temple court, the people were waiting for the priest to emerge after he offered the sacrifice to God and to bless them. Thus the atmosphere was one of devotion

---

[3] There were twenty-four courses into which the thousands of priests were divided. In addition to the three chief festivals of worship, each priestly section was assigned one week twice in the year to perform the Temple rites. Lots had to be drawn to determine which men would preside at the morning and evening sacrifices. The priest could have this honor but once in his lifetime, and many never received it.

and prayer.

Zechariah had not neglected his own spiritual preparation. He had been praying, certainly for a son. He had not despaired of fulfillment of his longing, although Elizabeth was beyond the normal childbearing years; but his hopes had grown thin. When the angel was discerned in the smoky mists of the room, his first word was to calm the priest's fears and then declare, "your prayer is heard." Zechariah would have his son, but the predictions of God's messenger were quite as startling. His child had been chosen for a unique role in God's eternal purpose.

The response of the angel leads to the supposition that the prayer concerns of Zechariah had gone beyond his own dreams and embraced the deep longings of the nation. He had dared to keep alive that yearning, almost abandoned, which had sustained Israel through the centuries—the Messiah's reign. At last Jehovah was about to act, and John, the priest's promised son, would be a part of the divine scheme. The significance of the name *John* is "Jehovah is gracious." This was the theme of the angelic prophecy, as well as Zechariah's response after the birth.

John's lot as Forerunner and his assignment in preparation for Messiah's way were explicit. The angel affirmed that he would "make ready for the Lord a people prepared" (Luke 1:17). In the father's outburst of praise when the boy was named, he spoke of the graciousness of God, who had remembered his covenant and visited again his people. The aging priest dedicated his son to "go before the Lord to prepare his ways, to give knowledge of salvation to his people in the forgiveness of their sins" (Luke 1:76-77).

How long a time John remained at home cannot be determined. Luke summarized perhaps three decades in one sentence (Luke 1:80). It is likely that he spent his formative years in the Judean household and that his father and mother were faithful to the strict Nazarite vows under which he was given to them. This would predispose John to a disciplined, even Spartan, life-style.

When he took up his residence in the desert hills around Hebron, the transition was easy and further qualified him as one with "the spirit and power of Elijah" (Luke 1:17). It may well have been that the death of his parents was the occasion for his wilderness training. Yet it could have been the compulsion of his inner urge to preach his unique message that drove him to the place of solitude and contemplation.

There he prepared—and waited. He would not speak out until all the characters of the drama were in place. Other events were in the making in Nazareth to the north. Then, with Jesus waiting in the wings, God would give the signal.

THE HANDMAID OF THE LORD

God had been working his plan in Nazareth as well as in Judea. The angel Gabriel fulfilled his function as a celestial messenger, to reveal and reassure. He is identified by Luke as being the angel who addressed both Zechariah and Mary. It was his lot to stand in the presence of the Lord (Luke 1:18), and with divine authority he announced that the time was at hand for the royal birth. The Gospel narratives never mute that dominant theme—the King is to be born! Even in the context of the tenderest of human experiences, the birth of a baby, the angel of God employed regal language in the startling disclosure to the young virgin. "He will be great . . . the Lord God will give to him the throne . . . he will reign . . . of his kingdom there will be no end" (Luke 1:32-33).

The essential message to Mary was not just that she was going to have a child. It was that this unique birth was to be the occasion of God's entry onto the human scene and into history! The heavenly representative seemed to hasten from the surprising news that Mary would conceive and, in the same sentence, hurried to the fact of who the babe would be. His name was given immediately, a procedure which normally waited to be considered at birth. The son was to be called Jesus, "Jehovah is salvation," because that was the sole purpose of the entire miraculous happening. The New Testament does not magnify the birth of a baby but the birth of a Savior!

Therein lies the peculiar hazard of the nationalization of Christmas. There may be only weariness and dread on the part of some that "Christmas has come"; the joy is when "Christ has come." The public easily borrows the thrill which accompanies the experience of reality, but a major fraction misses the experience itself. It would be futile to try to feel the "Spirit of '76" if there had been no revolution, or the spirit of romance if one is not in love with a person. The celebration of the birth of the Savior must embrace his saving work, all the way to his resurrection. Whoever would rejoice at God's gift must accept that gift. Otherwise the pageantry is empty, even obscuring the truth. One does not honor the birthday of Lincoln by trying to visualize the events of his babyhood or dramatize the crib on which he was laid. He is depicted, rather, as the gaunt and tortured president who agonized over the fate of the nation. No memorial to Pasteur attempts to reconstruct the events of his mother's delivery or his father's pride. He is recognized as one who gave life to many because of the antirabies vaccine he devised. Who individuals are and what they do become the occasions of their honors. Birth is but an essential entry to their destinies.

It is no wonder that the angelic herald, the night of Christ's birth, did not identify the occasion of joy as the news that a baby had been born. The declaration was: "For to you is born this day in the city of David a Savior, who is Christ the Lord" (Luke 2:11). If the King is born, then speak of his kingdom; if a Savior, sing of his salvation!

Yet it is appropriate to consider the young woman who did, indeed, conceive and bear a son. No one knew any better than she the implications of a virgin with child. At the instant of the angel's incredible announcement, the first picture to flash in her mind was her unmarried state. She went straight to that point with God's messenger. And very soon she had to face the prospect of her loneliness, her credibility with her parents, her explanations to Joseph, the leer of the skeptic, and the rage of the villagers who could invoke the death penalty by stoning for pregnancy out of wedlock.

Luke told her story sympathetically, and it is worth noting that he, a physician, should narrate the events of the conception.[4] So many intimate details and private thoughts are revealed that he must have had conversations with Mary herself. This is in keeping with the evangelist's own disclosure of the methods of research he used to secure his information. His sources were basically "eyewitnesses," and he claimed to have "followed all things closely" (Luke 1:1-4). There is one logical time span when interviews between the mother of Jesus and the doctor could have been held. Luke was in Caesarea with Paul during the apostle's two-year imprisonment there (see Acts 24:27). He was free to circulate in Galilee and Judea to search out the persons and places which were associated with the human life of Jesus. One can believe that Mary would have been glad to divulge those details to a physician who actually believed her story.

The New Testament places the chief emphasis not on any state of Mary's but on God's act. The divine plan called for God to fully manifest himself in human flesh. The Savior-King would be born of woman and fashioned out of the molecules of flesh and fiber. Such a person could then represent mankind and would be able to identify with every person in any condition of life or death, because he was born and lived and was tempted "as we are." Yet this mediator between God and man must also be free from any stain of sin and thus be the reconciling agent between God and mankind. Jesus' perfect sacrifice fully met the

---

[4] It should be remembered that the Roman Catholic doctrine of "the immaculate conception of Mary" does not refer to the moment when Jesus was conceived by the "power of the Most High" that overshadowed her (Luke 1:34). It is the position that Mary herself was conceived free from the stain of original sin.

needs of humanity as well as the terms of God's holy love. That kind of Savior was acceptable to both; and such a Messiah was fit to be the sovereign of all who would come freely into his kingdom.

Who is disposed to limit God at the apex of his purpose to redeem the race? If he is the omnipotent Creator, would he scruple to perform a simple act of creation in the crucial events toward which all history had been moving? In the formless void of space, in the unspeakable darkness before the universe existed, the Lord God created a sun. Is this an act too much for him simply because the human mind cannot conceive of a star ninety-three million miles from earth, which has for unknown centuries flamed in hydrogen explosions at thousands of degrees centigrade? If the nature of God as personality was fulfilled in fashioning other personalities to have fellowship with him, is the complexity of the human psychology and physiology thereby sufficient cause to declare the Almighty impotent to create life? And as for miracle, who does not stand in awe at the incredible succession of natural processes which produce even normal human birth?

The predominant reaction to the scriptural revelation is not the abundance but the severe economy of miracles. God seems always to prefer natural phenomena as long as these are available. Miracles appear to cluster at the crucial places in the Father's disclosure of himself and his plans. The appearance of God in the flesh, incarnation, is the premiere of such occasions. It was totally within the power and purpose of God for his Spirit, in that instance, to act with creative energies. The cardinal issue in Mary's conception is positive, not negative. It was not the absence of an earthly father but the overshadowing *presence* of the divine Father! The substitution was fitting because he who was to be born belonged to a higher sphere, and the forces resident in humanity alone were insufficient to produce him.

"BEACHHEAD AT BETHLEHEM"

It is useful, when truth is obscured by trivia, to crystallize great ideas and put them in perspective. Few issues need to be restated as urgently as those involved with the Advent of Jesus Christ. God created his universe and peopled it with creatures made in his personality image. He has not and will not yield his crown-rights as sovereign. Yet mankind willfully spoiled the design and severed the relationship. There was open rebellion, and civil war raged in the moral universe; but God was determined to put matters right again. Through the evidences in nature, the prodding of implanted conscience, and an increasing, continuous revelation, God had unceasingly pressed his claims on those he made to be his sons and daughters. But they were living in enemy-occupied territory, exactly as many Europeans were during the Nazi regime. When the time was ripe, the sovereign of history, the rightful King, landed on the human plane—made a beachhead at Bethlehem! In disguise as a newborn babe at first, he soon manifested his true identity, raised his banner, and summoned mankind to his cause in the counterrevolution and establishment of his kingdom. Only a view of such magnitude is sufficient to represent the true significance of the nativity story.

One of Christianity's most difficult assignments is to persuade people that history is not merely on a horizontal plane—that is, it does not merely concern what people do to people. The nucleus of God's redemptive plan is that God invaded history and became visibly active in its processes—the verticle plane. He is still thus engaged, and his kingdom is his primary vehicle for involvement with all his people. It was a bold concept that the invisible God, who is Spirit, should be incarnate and identify with his people as is common to all humanity—by being born as a baby.

The New Testament is the sole narrator of the events, and the first Gospel introduces the story with "Now when Jesus was born in Bethlehem of Judea" (Matt. 2:1). It may be helpful to reverse the words and reconstruct what can be known as to "when *was* Jesus born in Bethlehem?" Fact has almost been buried under the accumulation of legend and tradition and romance. Christians ought to be able to separate fact from fiction in regard to the time and circumstances of the birth of Jesus. Investigation mixed with caution can restore a measure of reality to the storied event.

Jesus was not born in A.D. ("the year of our Lord") 1 or 0. Ancients were unskilled and unscientific in the measurement of time or the design of calendars. Since there was no universal departure point, time was calculated by national landmarks or the reigns of monarchs and dynasties. Roman time prevailed in New Testament days and for six centuries thereafter. The best calculations place the date of Jesus' birth at AUC[5] 747 to 749. When Dionysius Exiguus was commissioned in A.D. 525 to convert the calendar, with the Advent of Christ as the beginning point, he miscalculated the death of Augustus Caesar by about five years. Thus, translated to the Christian scheme, the birthdate of Jesus is probably A.D. 4 or 5.

It is unlikely that the month was December and would be highly coincidental if the day were the twenty-fifth. By all evidence, shepherds were not in the fields from about November to March because of the rainy season; in cold weather the flocks were sheltered and fed in the folds. Herod would have had discretion as to when to implement Caesar's enrollment decree, and it was customary in such cases to conform to the best travel season in the several provinces. December was only one of numerous dates[6] suggested by the early church fathers. The first specific reference to December 25 is in a Latin monograph on the authority of Bishop Liberius, A.D. 354, which said that Christ was "born on the 25th of December, a Friday, and on the 15th day of the new moon." The day was arbitrarily chosen for symbolic reasons.

---

[5]*Ab Urbe Condita*, "from the founding of the city"—referring to Rome.
[6]Others were: January 5, March 28, April 20, May 20, and November 17.

The festivals of Mithra, goddess of light, influenced the calculators in selecting the twenty-fifth as being the darkest day of the year (as they believed); thus the light would thereafter triumph over darkness. It is now known that the twenty-first is nearer the date of the winter solstice. It is almost fruitless to try to identify the actual day. Any period of the summer or fall would be a good guess. The matter is immaterial, since the Scriptures show no interest in "times and seasons" because of man's inclination to formally observe the season and neglect the reality it represents.

It may be assumed that Mary did not give birth almost immediately after Joseph's hurried arrangements with an innkeeper for their lodging, as is so often depicted by legend. That is the type of drama which the New Testament recorder was not likely to miss. Rather, it is specifically stated that "while they were there, the time came for her to be delivered" (Luke 2:6). Nor is there any biblical mention of "midnight" or of the child's being born at night. Indeed, the angel said to the shepherds, "to you is born this day . . . a Savior" (Luke 2:11). The shepherds were visited at night—possibly in early evening since there is no hint that they were asleep—and they went immediately to the village to find the newborn babe. Certainly the courtesy of visiting the mother in the hours before normal time for retirement would have been extended by these men. The logical sequence would be for the birth to have occurred around noon or thereafter; then the mother would have had time for the necessary postnatal attention and the preparation of the baby. The shepherds would have been most welcome as evening callers, especially since they bore further news of heavenly involvement which only Mary and Joseph knew. These humble men were the first human encouragement they had since the visit to Elizabeth.

The record of the activities of the magi is probably the most intriguing of the Advent episodes (Matt. 2:1-18). These "Wise Men," as the biblical word is translated in most English versions, were of a priestly tribe of Medians who exercised great influence in the Persian empire. Teachers of religion and science, especially astronomy, they were honored scholars and considered to be of elevated character. It is likely that they lived in Persia or Babylonia. Herodotus, the most celebrated Greek historian who lived in the latter part of the fifth century B.C., testified to their role in foreseeing and interpreting special events. Their action in seeking out and paying homage to the newborn King was in keeping with their traditions. Seneca, the first-century Roman philosopher, told of magi who went to Athens to offer sacrifice to Plato, who had already died when they arrived. Cicero referred to a constellation of stars at the birth of Alexander the Great by which magi foretold the coming of one who was to be "the destroyer of Asia." It is probable that Matthew's narration of their visit to Bethlehem is deliberate evidence of the royalty of the infant Messiah, since the pilgrimage of such esteemed men would be a most impressive tribute.

Contrary to the lore of carol and pageant, the magi were not kings; there were quite possibly not three of them; and they did not cross the vast desert following the star. The appearance of the natal star was the occasion of research and calculation. Having concluded what the star portended, they determined to go to Jerusalem. There is no evidence that the star guided them. To the contrary, it probably shone for a period, then disappeared. Thus, on arriving in the city of the Jews, they had no further direction. Their question was "Where is he who has been born?" Then, having learned that Bethlehem was the place of prophecy, they took up the last six miles of their journey—and lo, at that point they saw the star again. They recognized it as the star they saw "in the East"—in the Eastern country where they resided, not in the eastern sky. They first saw its light in the western sky. This new certainty logically gave hope to their quest, and it was at this fresh guidance that they "rejoiced exceedingly with great joy." This would have been an impossible outburst if they had sighted it in the heavens nightly for months.

The number three has been assigned to the Wise Men because three gifts are identified. This is arbitrary, since their treasures were in gold and spices as was often true of the Oriental who traveled, taking his assets with him. The long desert trek strongly suggests there was a caravan, with many attendants—not three lone men on such an arduous and dangerous journey. Having found the child, they worshiped him. Giving of their treasure was their way of showing honor to the King-to-be and joy at the privilege accorded them. (See Gen. 43:11 and 1 Kings 10:2.)

The tradition of the magi's being thought of as kings is possibly derived from two passages in the Old Testament, from which no inference relating to the magi should be made. It is, of course, probable that these astrologers had the Jewish sacred books since they lived in the area where Judah was captive to Babylon. It is even possible that they had read "And nations shall come to your light, and kings to the brightness of your rising" (Isa. 60:3) or "Because of thy temple at Jerusalem kings bear gifts to thee" (Ps. 68:29). Had they identified such prophecies with the starry phenomenon they had observed, the combination may have spurred their decision to join a noble train of worshipers; but they had no thought of themselves as kings.

The magi proved themselves, indeed, as men of wisdom. Having only the most elemental evidence that an event had taken place worthy of an adventure of faith, they undertook a life-changing pilgrimage. They had read correctly whatever Scriptures they had and were eager to accept the acts of God as cause for action and allegiance: "For we . . . have come to worship him." The Jewish teachers of religion, on the other hand, were not nearly so perceptive. They had had the books of the covenant for generations and spoke often of the day when the Messiah would begin his reign. Yet despite prophecy and the high anticipation of the magi, they made no move to test whether these things might be so. The men from Babylon knew Jehovah but indistinctly, perhaps even intuitively. The scribes and priests walked daily in the Temple precincts, the holy place which served as a constant reminder that God was with his people. These had no eyes with which to see at the same moment when foreigners were beholding the climax of God's plan for the ages.

Their shortsightedness was prophetic of what was to come.

III
Jesus Came Preaching
The Manifesto of the King

*"Jesus came into Galilee, preaching the gospel
of God, and saying, 'The time is fulfilled, and
the kingdom of God is at hand; repent and
believe in the gospel.' " (Mark 1:14-15)*

A Galilean listening to Jesus, his fellow townsman, in his early
preaching ministry might have remarked, "I've heard that sermon
before." Had that citizen recently visited the region about the
Jordan he might very well have done so. John the baptizer "went
into all the region" (Luke 3:3) calling the Jews to repentance
and creating excitement wherever he set up a preaching station.
Evidently he began his proclamation in the wilderness area of
Judea, but began to work his way up the Jordan valley, where
he could find water to baptize the throngs which followed him.
His message hammered at a single concept: the kingdom of heaven
was at hand, and the way to enter it was to repent (Matt. 3:2,5,6).

How far north along the river John ventured cannot be determined. Already by the year A.D. 250 the location of "Bethany
beyond the Jordan" (John 1:28) had been lost, as the writer Origen
testified. Certainly it was not too far for John the Baptist to be
kept under the close scrutiny of the Jewish authorities. They sent
investigating committees time and again to interrogate him. Nev-
ertheless, the Galileans had close communication with Judea and
the well-traveled roads gave them access to major events and
ideas (see John 4:45). They had not missed the furor created by
the appearance of the rugged man from the desert.

So when they heard another evangelist, this time one of their
own, introducing the same kingdom and broadcasting the strange-
sounding doctrine of repentance, it was evident to them that there
were two voices but one theme. There is a remarkable but expected
harmony between the preaching of John and Jesus. These two

43

kinsmen, both around thirty (Luke 3:23), were of similar metal but cast in different molds. The baptizer was unconventional, severe, sensational, judgmental. Jesus appeared in clothing and demeanor as one of them, and by his wisdom he soon became known as "the teacher." So ordinary was he in physical aspects that Luke, the investigator, commented on the public view at the time Jesus began his ministry. So far as Galilee was concerned he was, as was supposed, "the son of Joseph" (Luke 3:23; Matt. 13:55). Indeed, on his first preaching attempt in Nazareth, the city of his childhood, the townspeople seemed to be startled at his profound and charming words. They thought highly of him since he had no doubt lived in an exemplary manner in his youth; but inevitably the tendency, then and now, was to be surprised that the hometown product could be exceptional. The term they used of his discourse in their synagogue, "gracious words," literally means that he had the indefinable gift of "charisma" (Luke 4:21-24). All his life people would be awed at the winsome manner of his speech as well as its profound contact.

PREPARATION FOR THE TASK

It is probable that everyone who studies the life of Jesus is intrigued by the biblical silence regarding his early years. The formative boyhood period out of which the man was made is a closed book, except for a single glimpse. Whatever was the traditional upbringing in a devout Jewish home no doubt was his as well. There can be little question but that Mary and Joseph felt themselves under strictest obligation to train the boy in the traditions of Israel, in the disciplines of the synagogue, and in the books of the law, the prophets, and "the writings." Luke alone alluded to the years between three and twelve in his familiar summary, "And the child grew and became strong, filled with wisdom; and the favor of God was upon him" (Luke 2:40).

One cannot help but wonder at the beginnings of his consciousness of who he was! This is a natural aspect of the growth of the ego, the emergence from infancy into self-awareness and identity. Every child is absorbed with this process of self-discovery. The adopted boy or girl begins to ask questions. The eager lad begins the mental adventure of what he is going to be. The little girl early identifies her doll and playthings as prototypes of her own home and baby. It is not a rare thing to find a minister of the gospel who has held the thoughts of this calling since the first days of his schooling. A boy or girl of ten or twelve can have a profound relationship to God.

It is purely conjecture, of course, that the young boy Jesus, hearing of the acts of God concerning his earthly forefathers, was so fascinated by the works of the Almighty that something began to stir in his nature—and his messianic consciousness dawned. It must not have come full blown, since the Bible takes care to state specifically that he grew, and that he "increased in wisdom" (Luke 2:52).[1] He was well advanced in his awareness by the time he reached the age of twelve. As some children spend hours reading and tinkering out of their love of science or mechanics or music, so must the boy Jesus have searched the Scriptures at the synagogue. An idea was growing in his mind, an insatiable hunger for more knowledge deep within his heart. The spirit of God was uniquely with him; and on a day which undoubtedly he remembered, his eyes opened wide with a burst of understanding! *He* was the Messiah! It was he, himself, about whom the Scriptures spoke! From that moment onward, Jesus of Nazareth, as boy and man, pressed toward the knowledge of the will of his Father—and did it. It would be eighteen years before he declared his true nature, but he already knew.

Against some such background one comprehends better the significance of Luke's record of the visit of young Jesus to Jerusalem (Luke 2:41-51). It was his first Passover after he was eligible to observe the ordinances. At twelve he became "a son of the

---

[1] For further comment on Jesus and learning, see Hebrews 5:8,9, remembering that the word "perfect" means full-grown.

law," admitted to the privileges of the covenant. The central point is not the search of the parents for a missing son, although that is illuminating. It is that the lad was utterly preoccupied with his first opportunity, outside his own synagogue, to hear the great rabbis expound on the law of God. He was hungry to learn. Everything was not yet clear to him, and a thousand questions tugged at his mind. It is not surprising that Luke identified the pivotal scene in the vignette. The Jewish elders and teachers were giving public instruction, probably on a porch or terrace in the Temple precincts. Seated with others on the ground before them the boy was lost in rapt attention, "listening to them and asking them questions." He was caught up in eternal things, and time had ceased to have meaning.

There is obviously no record of the questions he put to these learned scholars, but it can be surmised that he focused on issues which related to his own growing convictions. It was no time for him to be speculative or philosophical. Was he not concerned with the nature and conditions of God's covenant with his people? Was the law adequate to realize the purpose of Jehovah? Had the prophetic moment come near when a new covenant should be written in the heart? How did they interpret the nature and reign of the Messiah?

At any rate he respectfully gave attention; and when they answered question with question, the boy startled them all with his grasp and comprehension of the Scriptures. The verb "were amazed" connotes repeated astonishment. And when Mary and Joseph located him, they too joined in the wonder at what they saw and probably at what they heard—if they waited a while before Mary claimed her son and remonstrated with him. A clue is furnished in Jesus' response to his mother's reproach. It might well indicate the immediate context of the dialogue just concluded. Certainly it revealed where his mind was at that moment. Enigmatically he asked how it was so difficult to locate him. Should not they have expected him to be in "my Father's house"? It is probable that he placed vocal stress on "my Father's," looking them full in the eye. He intended for it to be a significant phrase and a meaningful glance. At that instant he must have felt a surge of certainty that God was uniquely his Father. The innuendo was not lost on the parents. That "they did not understand" is evidence that they sensed his deeper meaning. It was just one more thing that Mary had to ponder in her heart.

It is nearly certain that things at home in Nazareth were different after the encounter in the Temple. Jesus was a dutiful son, but a new factor had entered into the purely parent-child relationship. The boy was aware of his unique role, and that fact must have intruded into every conversation, act of discipline, and plan for the family future. One wonders, even, if Mary might have been moved by the occasion to decide that it would not be long before she must divulge to Jesus the events of his birth. It was inevitable that the day would come when she would call him aside and open with some such query as, "Son, you know there is something unusual about you, do you not?" He had a right to know.

The general supposition is that Joseph died during the eighteen years that intervened before Jesus manifested himself. So the growing young man busied himself with the responsibilities as the elder son of a household where there were then at least six other children (Matt. 13:55-56). He was necessarily senior in the affairs of the family carpentry shop. Nonetheless, these crucial years were the time of final preparation for his ministry. As duties would allow, he had to spend long segments of time alone. Solitude was essential to his understanding of himself and his task. He walked in the fields, where he stored up the rich reserves of nature lore which served him so well in his parables—birds, flowers of the field, hay and stubble, the farmer sowing, the servant plowing, shepherds tending the flocks, the mean-spirited landholder who built great barns, laborers in the vineyards. His eye measured carefully the life of his village and the numerous surrounding

Galilean towns. As he took part in the normal life of the day, he observed children in the marketplace, slaves and masters, faithful and unfaithful servants, Jew versus Samaritan, the scramble for the best seats at the banquet, a son who went away into a far country, pearl merchants, marriage feasts, and fishermen. All these he wove into the colorful fabric of his teaching and opened uncomprehending minds with the words, "Now the kingdom of heaven is like . . . ."

As the time drew near, for rabbis customarily showed themselves at around age thirty, he knew the way he must go. The hours of meditation and his prayers with the Father had fully prepared him. Even the sure knowledge that death alone could be the end of such a reversal of Jewish tradition did not daunt him from his course. He was not just a man who aspired to authority; he was the Son of God. His nature was God's nature, and he was the King who must advance to establish and claim his realm. Necessity was upon him; and when the news from Judea began to filter into Galilee, it stirred him to action. His distant cousin, John (and did not Mary also tell Jesus about Elizabeth and her son?), was declaring that the kingdom of heaven was about to appear and telling the nation that one "mightier than I is coming." Jesus knew who that was, and he was ready. So the day came when the man of Nazareth gathered his earthly family, bade them good-bye, and set out to invite all mankind into the family of God.

What Shall We Do?

It is beyond doubt that the first word of the gospel was *repent!* Only a notion so radical as a complete change of attitude and action would be effective for men who already considered themselves members of God's kingdom. If there was to be a new kind of kingdom, then the terms of entry had to be clearly drawn. Both Forerunner and Messiah gave primacy to that. And, as if to accent the abandonment of the old system, John and Jesus introduced a baptismal rite which the believer openly received as evidence of his new allegiance.

Clearly it was a bewildering experience for those who first heard the preaching of so strange a gospel. Whoever comprehended the issue was aware that such a kingdom would nullify their centuries-long dependence on the Mosaic law to satisfy the demands of God. The priesthood was at once confronted with a challenge to their role as administrators of the ritual system. Here was an uncouth, itinerant desert prophet admitting men of the Jewish commonwealth to a unique realm of God—and by whose authority? The more perceptive of their leaders were sure to conclude in time that the invitation they heard with their own ears along the Jordan was bound to include Gentiles. Indeed, soldiers (and these might be Roman) were already responding, as were tax collectors—and that was quite as intolerable. Official opposition, therefore, to the proclamation of "a baptism of repentance" (Luke 3:3) was inevitable.

Multitudes, however, were disposed to believe, and the popularity of the new movement spread. Even though "repent and believe" fell on unpracticed ears, they heard the message that *action* was required of them. The question was "What then shall we do?" (Luke 3:10), illustrating the fact that they never had to *do* anything before. Born as Israelites, they had from birth been included in the covenant God made with their forefathers. It was theirs to know and obey the law and follow the rituals of sacrifice. What more could be required of a son of Abraham?

But now a premium was placed on a mighty act of the will. Both mind and heart had to undergo a change; there had to be a choice, a self-declaring. Nothing in religion like that had ever been demanded before. Whatever changes had previously been effected had been quantitative—doing more. This time the quality of faith was to be startlingly different. Focus would be on the individual, not his heritage; on experience, not performance; on creativity, not obedience.

This revolutionary concept in religion is contained in the Greek word universally used in the New Testament for repentance—*metanoia*. Although it is intimately connected with confession and forgiveness of sin, it contains far more than the traditional definition as being "sorrow for sin." The literal meaning of the term is "change the mind." Emotions are inseparable from the kind of change intended, but repentance can never be limited to an emotional response. Something more permanent than transient human feelings is involved.

Repentance consists in a radical transformation of thought, attitude, disposition, and direction. A turning is central to the idea (this was the significance of the doctrine in the Old Testament) and is continuous in nature. Indeed, nothing short of a revolution in personality is called for. An ingredient in this new awareness is godly sorrow. Inevitably, one who experiences such a vital new relationship with God and man will have a deep sense of grief at the former condition as well as a surge of joy in the new state.

For the purposes of the kingdom of heaven the total personality involvement in repentance is all-important. The aim of Jesus in his new realm was not the heart or the head of the believer, but the whole man. The implications of "changing the mind" are not at odds with such a goal. Common usage is an excellent illustration. One sits in a restaurant with a friend whom he has not seen for a while. He orders oysters. Remembering his former hatred of the taste of oysters, the friend chides him about the choice. "Oh," he replies, "I've changed my mind about oysters." Well, what has he changed? He has altered the way he *thought* about oysters, the way he *feels* about them, and the way he *acts* toward them. It was not merely an intellectual or emotional evaluation; it was a new disposition and a turning to a new way which is expected to continue. In the root sense of the Greek word, he had "repented" concerning oysters.

The growth of a kingdom where Christ rules in the lives of his followers will depend on the continuous aspect of the new

godly attitude. It has often been popular for a typical command
of a drill sergeant to be used to describe the state of those who
repent. To soldiers facing the line of march, the officer barks,
"About face!" The squad turns around to the opposite direction.
That, some have said, is repentance. But not quite. Something
has been omitted. Not until the command "Forward, march" has
been executed is the picture of repentance adequate. It does not
greatly matter which way a soldier is looking if he is not going
anywhere!

John the Baptist had not neglected the full application of this
cardinal doctrine. So when the people began to ask him what
they should do, he responded by giving them assignments which
were possible only in their new states, not the old. It was not
natural to give one of a man's two coats to him who had none.
It would have been unnatural for the tax collectors of the day
to charge only by the assessed values. They bought the lucrative
position of publican solely because it was the accepted practice
to collect from every individual as much as could be extracted.[2]
As for soldiers who lived by violence, how could they be expected
not to use violence on subject people? Clearly the sons of the
kingdom had to experience dramatic changes in the ways they
thought and felt and acted. They had to venture where they had
never walked before.

A valid concept of repentance is indispensable to Jesus' kind
of kingdom because it takes into consideration the source as well
as direction of change. Universally, religious systems had been
regulated by external force and authority. There was always a
hierarchy of some sort. A priesthood mediated between man and
the gods of primitive religions and also in case of Jehovah in
the Old Testament economy. Ranked above the priest was a
well-defined structure of power, culminating in an authoritative
religious personage or office. The laws and regulations and cultic

---

[2] Is it possible that a tax collector named Matthew was there on occasions
and heard this word?

practices were in every case imposed from either a book or code or tradition. Worship was prescribed in manner and time and place. Morals were regulated.

The kingdom of heaven is based on a revolutionary new concept. The believers themselves would qualify as the priesthood, each competent to handle the sacrifice Christ made once for all. No man would superintend another man's soul. The Christian is not to be justified by satisfaction of the law; he or she is in a creative relationship with the Lord himself, who teaches and guides and disciplines his friends. No one can tell the disciple how to worship or authorize the place. How each one is to live is determined through interpreting the Scriptures and out of the dialogue of prayer. It is no wonder, then, that the driving force for the kingdom man must be from within. That is where the change occurs; the whole person becomes new. There is no provision for any other motivating factor imposed from without. Jesus underscored that truth. When Pharisees asked him when the kingdom of God was coming, the Lord warned them not to look for external sign or evidence. "For, behold," he declared, "the kingdom of God is within you" (Luke 17:21, KJV).

Committed to His Kingdom

The mechanics of inner commitment are so indefinable and intensely personal that they do not lend themselves to verification, except at long-range observation. What, indeed, causes a man to "make up his mind"? Yet life pivots on just such fragile decisions. The quiet change is made deep within, and the future takes another direction. Belief in Christ and acceptance of the claims of his kingdom originate in that unspectacular way. Yet, because allegiance to his reign is not merely a private matter, and since discipleship is not secret, the believer is called upon for an open declaration. Baptism, to the Christian, is putting on the uniform of membership in the kingdom of heaven. Baptism, for Christ, was more the confirmation of the King.

Jesus was not baptized by John in the Jordan because he repented. Why then? It was for himself, in part, because it was his dedication to giving life to mankind by his own death, burial, and resurrection. This was the way to his dominion. His subjects were to be those who, by belief in him, died to the bondage of sin and were buried, death having done all it could do. But then, as Jesus came up out of the water, it was a promise of his being raised as victor over death. Clearly he who conquered death would have authority to rule, and the open approval of the voice from heaven vindicated his claim to be the Son of God. He would be worthy of his throne by his own supreme sacrifice. Kingdom men would be alive by the same power that caused their Lord to live.

But Jesus was baptized by John, and in so doing he authenticated the acts and claims of John the Baptist. He had made baptism a sign of Christ's kingdom even before the death and resurrection of the Lord gave fullest meaning to the ordinance. Was this a valid rite for the Forerunner? Where and how did John conceive this symbolic ceremony? There was no clear precedent in Judaism. Jewish proselyte [3] baptism was merely a purification ritual after circumcision that had no actual documentary evidence until the fifth century. It grew up after the destruction of the Temple in Jerusalem as a symbol of entrance into Judaism. The proselyte stood in the water and dipped himself. Since the Temple stood in John's day and ceremonial acts were performed there, there is no reason to believe that immersion practices existed prior to the preaching in the desert. It is not mentioned in the Old Testament, in the rabbinical writings, in Philo or Josephus, or in any of the apocryphal books.

It must have been, then, that John had divine insight in his wilderness training. Under God's tutelage he saw in his mind's eye a dramatic act of individual commitment that could not be

---

[3] Converts to Judaism from other races or religions.

lightly accepted. It symbolized to him the new mind toward God and a confession of sin. It is doubtful that he could have known the richness of meaning that the Christ would pour into it by dying and being raised from the grave. Jesus attested to John's role as the voice of prophecy of his coming and authenticated the practice of baptism, which he continued through his apostles.

THE KING ON TRIAL

It was a high moment for Jesus as he departed from the scene of his open declaration that his time had come. The long years of readying for his ministry were past. He had been certified by the Father; how should he go about establishing his kingdom? What strategy must he adopt that would summon believers on terms that could accomplish the definitions in his own mind of what kind of kingdom it was to be? Before he asked the first individual to join his enterprise he would have to resolve those issues. So, as his pattern had been and was to be, he sought solitude. There he could commune with the only one who could give him counsel.

Between the Judean plateau, on which Jerusalem was built, and the valley of the Dead Sea, there stretched a tortured and desolate waste, some 525 square miles in expanse. It was blistered by the sun, devastated by drouth and erosion, desolate and foreboding. Its rocky hills thrust up in irregular barren peaks and then fell away abruptly toward the salt sea below. There a man could be alone, and there Jesus went to ponder and pray. He did not resort to a device in order to be tempted to create a charade. His was no act in which he toyed with Satan's wiles, smiling all the while because he had seen the script. Unless he was sorely tried because he wanted the kind of prizes the devil offered, then the temptation was not real at all; and he would be suspect as a human and as Messiah.

At the core of this testing of his messiahship was his longing to win men to his kingdom. The timing was right, just as has always been experienced by Christians. Still with the glow of the Father's approval, he was an excellent psychological target for the tempter. In the deep introspection about his methods, he was ripe for suggestions as to ways which seemed immediately productive but which masked their ultimate peril. He had, so far as is known, never used his supernatural powers. Could he? What rights did he have because of his unique sonship? A hungry man would sooner or later think of bread. A king utterly alone would aspire to a realm. The Son of God would be susceptible to the notion that he could command angels. Thus the ingredients of the trial were present, and Jesus had the untried powers inherent in his nature. The question was, how would he use them?

The six weeks Jesus spent in intense introspection and prayer took its toll. The mental and spiritual strain naturally dulled his appetite. There was nothing in that hostile environment to make him think of food. And the consequent weakness presented to Satan a unique opportunity to put Jesus' humanity to a severe test.

The desert floor was scattered with small flat, oval stones which were remarkably shaped and colored like the pancake-size loaves in which the bread of Jesus' era was baked. He must have rested one day after his long fast, and while seated on an outcropping of rock his eyes chanced to fall upon some of those stones. In his imagination he saw them as the crusty loaves he had known at his mother's table only two months before. They looked like bread slices, and he wanted them! Moreover, it was right for him to satisfy his human instinct of hunger. Instantly the thought was in his mind: could he command the stone to become bread? Should he? To the first question, he would have answered affirmatively: yes, he had the power. And since his attention had been centered for so long on how to win men, a second idea must have followed logically—such miracles of provision would be an unbeatable way to call others to his service. If he fed the people, they would flock to him.

Immediately he discerned the true nature of what he was experiencing. It was a diabolical plot to get him to deny his manhood! His answer, probably given aloud in the instant of victory, was that of course he needed food, but would not under any circumstance prostitute his divine power for mere human appetite—his or any other man's! He accepted the limitations and obligations of his flesh, but he preserved the higher prize of his relationship to God. He would not, then or ever, exchange his godly responsibilities for material ends. It was a genuine temptation. Had he not endured it, if he had been spared the trials of his flesh, any doctrine of Jesus as a real man would be a farce. Since he resisted, believers have a king, a Savior, and a friend who understands their humanity. He has the right to speak to the use of their bodies and appetites.

This first of three temptations recorded by Luke (Luke 4:1-13) sets the pattern for the other two. It is not necessary to suppose that the others followed immediately, but it is likely that they occurred close to the end of the retreat period in the wilderness area.[4] Satan would, of course, wait for the flush of triumph over the bread incident to wane. He likes to catch people in spiritual troughs. In his contemplative wanderings, Jesus must have come one day to one of the higher peaks in that Judean desert, where he could see in the far distance the evidences of empire and commerce and social life. In a mental picture he visualized all the kingdoms in the earth. Whenever he saw men, women, or children, his compassions stirred. He had created them for himself (see John 1:3), and he wanted them. He had an instinct for authority and rule based on love. But again, how could he constrain them to willingly come to him?

The tempter was prepared with another easy answer, now appealing to the legitimate human instinct for power. The devil claimed possession of world power, and Jesus did not deny that;

---

[4] Note that the order of the second and third temptations is reversed by Matthew and Luke. See Matthew 4:1-11.

but the Lord of all the earth did not concede that Satan was sovereign. Earthly dominion was not granted to the evil one, and his would not be the final victory. Therefore, there would be not even a slight acknowledgment of the satanic boast by any semblance of worship. That belonged only to the Lord God. This was a unique testing of Christ's messiahship. He came to win the world; but the conditions of his conquest were paramount. Had he recognized the devil's claim to mankind and dared to accept his methods, then there would have been no death struggle, no sacrifice by which he could have been worthy of the deep affections of his followers by reason of his complete self-giving. It was the temptation to the easy way. The Savior was now committed to the difficult but more permanent way. He was determined to struggle to keep men and women away from the evil one. No price was too high for him to pay. He had set his face on the hard way to the cross.

The third event in the temptation narrative has a different setting. It may be that Satan "took him to Jerusalem" in an imaginary fashion. Yet it is entirely possible that it represents a lonely visit to the city. It is probably nearing or at the end of the wearying forty-day period, and Jesus' mind had turned again toward people and association with them. He emerged from the desert and felt drawn to the Temple area, for the city was not far from the site of his solitary vigil. The Scriptures describe him as going on the "pinnacle" of the Temple. The word means "wing," probably one of the porches constructed high over the Kedron valley, a sheer wall nearly five hundred feet in height. Looking down, perhaps feeling some dizziness, the suggestion came to him that if he should jump, would not angels preserve him from otherwise certain death? As Son of God certainly he could claim the right to divine protection!

It was a natural thought, but the Master saw it for what it was—a denial of his relationship of faith with the Father. It was an attempt to destroy his sonship, just as the two previous ones had been attacks on his humanity and his messiahship. To fall in line with Satan's wishes would have been a gross distortion of faith, a rejection of spiritual things. It was the temptation to presumption! It can be made to look and sound strangely like faith. As in all other instances, the matter of winning disciples was a central issue. The Jewish teachers had most often described the coming of Messiah in cataclysmic terms. If he should appear in a physical descent from above, full in the public view, then surely it would have been a cause for belief that this was the coming one. Such a miracle would have had multitudes clamoring for his elevation to power. No, he would find another way to enter Jerusalem and the hearts of his people.

It is evident that Satan did not strike at the outer edges of Jesus' consecration to his kingdom purposes. He tried for the knockout blow. If he could lure the man of Nazareth to compromise before he openly manifested himself, then he would have nullified God's redemptive plan before it unfolded. It can be expected, then, that in his unceasing attacks on kingdom men he would not nibble at the margins but go for the core. Repeated assaults have been launched against the same vital sector. Disguises and weapons have varied through the ages, but the aim is the same. His names indicate that he is the adversary (Satan), the slanderer (devil). His bitter enmity is with the works of God, and he restlessly probes every weak spot of the Christian. He has been more successful with the Christian's church than with its Lord.

In every age, when his followers try to use the name of Christ for material advantage, they but resort to the folly of trying to turn stones into bread. If fleshly considerations take precedence over spiritual purpose, the same futile scheme is played out again. Let mankind accept the limitations of the flesh as the Master did and not give preeminence to desire. It is when one attempts to satisfy instincts and right desires in the wrong way that they become sins.

The church tried the way of compromise early in its history. In order to win converts, churchmen bowed down, only a little now and again, before Satan and heathen practices entered the doctrine and polity of medieval Christendom. The custom is not out of style. If the modern Christian does not fall down before the evil one, he tends to make ever-so-slight curtsies on occasions and listens to counsel on how to be popular and get a mass of people into the church. The way of the world is easy; its gimmicks are alluring, and its practitioners are quickly the envy of their peers. Jesus warned solemnly about the broad gate. It is deceiving. No one has ever discovered an easy way to change men *within* en masse. The way of repentance and personal choice and vital faith is slow and tortuous, but it is the effective way. And it is the way Jesus introduced his kingdom and set the example under trial.

Strangely enough, it remains a popular fashion to leap from the pinnacle of the Temple. Presumption is close to faith and wears its robes. The people of God too easily scorn the routine applications of faith and often are lured by sensation. Special favors from God are demanded as proof of his faithfulness. People put him to the test as though the Almighty must serve them on their own terms as the price of belief. When they dash their feet against the stones, faith falters and doubts grow. But sons of the kingdom recognize the Lord's preeminence and do not tempt him. Faith is to them the real bond of the Christian to his Lord, and its application to life is rarely spectacular. They have learned to live well like men while bearing in themselves the nature of God. From that kind of material Jesus Christ can fashion a kingdom.

IV
To Be with Him

The Citizens of the Kingdom

*"And he appointed twelve, to be with him, and
to be sent out to preach"* (Mark 3:14).

John the Baptist must have wondered where Jesus was when
he did not appear the day after his baptism. Surely he expected
the newly declared Son of God to begin preaching, perhaps even
alongside the Forerunner. Yet day after day passed with no word
as to his whereabouts, and this silence stretched into six weeks.
Only later, when Jesus himself probably shared the intimate and
sensitive experience with his friends, could anyone have known
that the Master had been fighting his own spiritual battles in
the Judean desert.

The baptizer, however, was daily at his appointed task. He had
not been relieved; therefore, he continued to be faithful. By that
time he had been several months in his ministry; and from among
the believers he had chosen certain ones to be his disciples, quite
probably his assistants in the work of baptizing. With these he
must have shared his understanding of the Messiah's arrival and
his own commission. Therefore, they were prepared for belief
and acceptance far beyond the others who first were introduced
to Jesus. The identity of only two of these men has been preserved:
Andrew of Bethsaida and a promising young convert with unusual
spiritual capacity. His name was John.[1]

It is not necessary to think of the disciples of John the Baptist
as present with him each day, as was also the case with Jesus'

---

[1] See John 1:35-40. From this point on, references to John the Baptist will
use his full name and office. Any mention of the name *John* alone will pertain
to this John, the disciple of the baptizer, who became the beloved apostle of
Jesus. He is also here accepted as the author of the Fourth Gospel.

disciples during the first year. So the likelihood is that Andrew and John were not on duty that noteworthy day when the baptizer looked up and "saw Jesus coming toward him" (John 1:29). In his relief at Jesus' reappearance, the Forerunner exclaimed for all to hear, "Behold, the Lamb of God, who takes away the sin of the world." Many eyes from among the congregation by the riverbanks turned to follow the Baptist's look, and possibly his gesture. These sons of Israel's covenant knew the significance of that kind of sacrificial lamb, but it was not possible for them to have grasped the meaning of the eloquent and prophetic tribute as applied to the person of Jesus.

Again on the next day Jesus appeared on the scene. But this time the two disciples of the Baptist were present. By their actions it may be concluded that they had a prearranged signal: the repetition of the same statement about the Lamb of God from the previous day. During the night the baptizer could have summoned them and joyfully declared that the one whom he had expected for so long had at last arrived. It was time for the two men to leave their first teacher and follow him for whom they were being prepared. It is not hard to imagine the anticipation of Andrew and John on that fateful day as they looked eagerly at every new face that joined the throng at the Jordan. Suddenly they saw John the Baptist gaze intently upon one young man and repeat the significant phrase. This was the one, and without further delay "they followed Jesus." They had been well prepared.

Jesus' first encounter with a follower is a winsome story, preserved in great detail by young John (he may have been no more than twenty), who shared the moment. To this point the Master had been terribly alone. With so much to say there had been no one with whom to share, except the Father. It would never be that way again. As a man, he needed people; as the Messiah, he had the urge to communicate. From this day on, therefore, he would have to seek solitude to escape the pressure of crowds. Except in prayer, he would never be alone again.

It is instructive to note the first recorded public words of Jesus Christ. We have his comment to his parents at age twelve, and he gave private instruction to the Forerunner about baptizing him; but there is no prior record of any public utterance. It is noteworthy that his opening sentence was to those who would be his friends and apostles and loyal subjects. As he walked past the gathered audience listening to the baptizer, he went on his way until he became aware that he was being followed. Turning, seeing the expectant look on the faces of the two men, he undoubtedly smiled to indicate acceptance and asked, "What do you seek?" His question would be equivalent to "What purpose do you have?" What kind of answer would be proper to such a question? They did the right thing; they tacitly invited themselves to go home with Jesus for a quiet conversation.

The first response of the Master to an approach was an invitation, and so it has forever been. They wanted to be with him, and he wanted them. So when they inquired as to where he was staying, his answer was a polite invitation: "Come and see." One could passionately wish it were possible to know where that was! He had not yet established a home base; there were no believers; so where did he lodge during these first few days? It was an introduction and a visit which made a deep impression on John. Writing perhaps fifty years later, he recalled that they spent the entire day with Jesus. Indeed, he even remembered the time of morning when they arrived. It was 10 A.M.

It took a long while for Jesus to make his first friends, but now a rapid progression took place. One told another of his discovery. The selections were not indiscriminate. There was no attempt to recruit from the public. It stood to reason that these first disciples approached only those in whom there was a pronounced spiritual readiness. Since so much had to be taken on faith, faith had to be already present. Of the several instances of how the story spread among the select few, one must be recounted. It brings into the picture a man whose name, along with John, ranks highest among those who joined their lives to the newfound King. His name was Simon Peter.

He was Andrew's brother; and they, along with Philip, who came into the band the next day, lived in the Galilean village of Bethsaida. After the hours with Jesus, Andrew, in his excitement, went immediately and found Simon, perhaps after a day in the fishing boats on the lake. His eager cry, "We have found the Messiah," indicates that the subject was a matter of lively interest between the brothers. Certainly Simon would have known of Andrew's association with John the Baptist, and it is logical to suppose that Simon himself had attended the preaching and teaching sessions. The wording of the statement that Andrew "brought him to Jesus" (John 1:42) suggests both that it was late in the day and that Peter might have had some reluctance to go immediately to meet the man responsible for his brother's enthusiasm.

The meeting between Jesus and Simon was significant. Jesus had probably heard of the fisherman, who was certainly not known for his reticence or modesty. The record states that Jesus looked intently at him—a kind of duel of the eyes, each man measuring the other. "So you are Simon?" he said, as though he had had reports on him. Somehow under that compelling gaze Simon had nothing to say, a rarity for him. One can only suppose that Jesus liked him and saw a potential for strength in him, since he gave him a prophetic name: Peter, the rock. In that moment the Lord depicted his entire purpose—to work a transformation in the natures of those who accepted him, on which he was to build the kingdom of heaven and his church.

THE MAKING OF DISCIPLES

If, indeed, "movements move on men," then it would be surprising if Jesus had not turned his attention first to those who would become a nucleus of his new kingdom. He would not always be physically present among his people, and he only had a limited period to prepare them for their tasks. The accounts of his early ministry, therefore, are chiefly concerned with the selection and training of the men, and later certain women, to whom he would entrust the expansion of his realm.

It was for them a painfully difficult transition. They had been schooled in the traditions of Israel; and although they were more perceptive than others in recognizing the Messiah, it remained true that they had to be retaught every step of the way. Their priests and scholars had anticipated no such manifestation of the "Coming One" as Jesus appeared to be. Therefore, the public accepted traditional messianic expectations: sudden, dramatic appearance, heroic governmental leadership, and a call to conquest, especially of the Roman oppressor. The early disciples had absorbed that mind-set, and Jesus had to deal gently with their slowly developing faith. They were frequently puzzled by what their Master said and did; their faith often faltered. Gradually they understood him more fully. He painstakingly taught them by word and deed. He demonstrated his authority as Lord over nature and mankind in unmistakable ways. Little by little they comprehended the nature of his kingdom. And in the remarkably brief space of less than three and one-half years, he had prepared a core of men and women who became the nucleus of a world-changing gospel.

The beginnings of Jesus' public ministry are but sketchily portrayed by the four Gospel narratives, chiefly by John. This early Judean period embraced some six to eight months.[2] He was based in unknown locations in northern Judea, usually near to the Jordan, with one excursion into Cana of Galilee for a well-defined reason. It is necessary to visualize him accompanied by five or six followers [3] who were not permanently with him. Clearly most of them

---

[2] Most of these events are contained only in John 1:29 to 4:54. The other three writers move quickly to the longer Galilean campaign, one-and-a-half years in length.

[3] Five of them have already been named: Andrew, John, Peter, Philip, and Nathanael. Many suppose that James, brother of John, was also included. See Mark 1:19.

were commercial fishermen on the nearby Sea of Galilee. The likelihood is that they served with him on occasions, and for varying lengths of time, while still earning their livelihood by the net.

The occasion which caused Jesus to visit briefly in Galilee is preserved by John (see John 2:1-11), who accompanied him along with some of his fellow disciples. There was a wedding in Cana, probably important to Jesus' family, and it seems clear that it was an engagement he had before he left home only a short time before. The important role played by Mary, his mother, suggests that the groom was a kinsman of Jesus. He took his newly found disciples along, and it could be that these extra houseguests caused the untimely failure of the supply of wine at the several days of feasting.

Mary, who seems to have been in charge, involved Jesus in a socially embarrassing situation with no advance notice. The presence of the five or six men who had accepted him as the Messiah may be the reason Jesus decided to work the miracle of providing wine from water. Consider how closely they must have watched him as he commanded the servants. They had never seen him use any powers above those of ordinary men. It is certain that they never forgot their amazement as the drinking vessels, filled with freshly drawn water, proved to contain wine which the toastmaster called "the good wine." It was convincing evidence to these men. They had believed in Jesus as much as they knew. Now there was more, much more. He had authority over nature; he had creative powers! Only God had such might; therefore, their Master must truly have been from God. The most important sentence in the narrative gives reason for this first miracle: "and his disciples believed in him." The first great lesson had been learned.

Immediately there followed a brief, but apparently happy, interlude. His own family had not yet turned against him, as they later did. So, along with the disciples, he joined his mother and brothers for a short sojourn in Capernaum (see John 2:12), likely with relatives. The picture of that reunion is suggestive. This was not his Nazareth home, but Capernaum would soon be his only real home for the rest of his ministry. These kinsmen were now his family, but soon would not be. Others who believed in him would be his family, and he would say so openly (Mark 3:31-35). He was in the process of creating a new concept—the family of God—another startlingly different feature of his kind of kingdom.

The coming of the time for the Jewish high feast of Passover called Jesus and his friends back to Jerusalem.[4] He himself observed this most sacred religious festival, but it was also a foreshadowing of his own sacrifice as "the Lamb of God." While performing the prescribed rituals in the Temple area, Jesus forced the traders and money changers out of the sacred precincts. This was yet another chapter in the disciples' education as they carefully put away in their minds these claims of authority over the house of God. Three years and more later, they "remembered" (John 2:17,22). Apparently his every action was not only to declare publicly who he was, but to persuade his first disciples that he was more than a man who was their friend.

Jesus and his band then returned to the Jordan area, where a vital part of the training period took place. They preached and baptized. This was the first opportunity the six had to actually declare their beliefs and recount their experiences. As often as they could be away from their fishing boats, they labored with Jesus not far from where John the Baptist was still summoning the people to repentance. Fortunately, John clearly states that these men actually did the baptizing for Jesus (John 3:22; 4:1-2). The wisdom of that is obvious; what a source of pride it might have become if some could have claimed to be immersed at the hands of the Lord himself!

[4] This feast recorded in John 2:13 is the first of the four Passovers noted by John. The others are in 5:1 (probably); 6:4; and 13:1. Were it not for these timetables, it would be impossible to establish the length of Jesus' preaching ministry—three and one-half years.

Abruptly, however, there was a change. The new movement had become too popular for the ruling religious leaders to tolerate longer. Action was taken for the first time; John the Baptist was arrested and imprisoned. And since Jesus and his men had gained an even more popular following than the Baptist, the attention of the Pharisees would soon be turned in that direction. The Lord knew it was not yet time for a showdown with Jerusalem, so he decided to move his scene of operations to Galilee. There, in the more liberal atmosphere of a province not dominated by Pharisee and Sadducee, he could declare his kingdom and teach his disciples.

The Base at Capernaum

It cannot be known whether Jesus might have selected Nazareth as his home base had the people there received him. He had come from Judea already widely acclaimed (Luke 4:14). So Jesus was no longer the boy and man who used to observe every sabbath in his accustomed place in the synagogue. He was a celebrity; and when the seventh day arrived, he was chosen to read the lesson and invited to speak. No wonder "the eyes of all in the synagogue were fixed on him" (Luke 4:20). He read an Isaiah passage which was highly appropriate for him, one filled with messianic language. The crowd was expectant; what would their now-famous townsman do with it? He left them not long in doubt. "Today this scripture has been fulfilled in your hearing." It was either the central truth of history or unprecedented arrogance. They were infuriated at his claim to be the Messiah, and murder was in their hearts. He only narrowly escaped being thrown headlong from a cliff at the southwest corner of the town.

When people rejected Jesus he left; it was his pattern. His time was short, and his kingdom was a rule of faith deep in the individual heart. Belief could not be coerced; it was each individual's responsibility to deny or accept him. So he went down to Capernaum on the northwestern shore of the Sea of Galilee and there set up his headquarters. It would be his home until some six months before his death.

It was inevitable that Jesus could not continue permanently with a volunteer system of followers. Too much would depend on them in the future. Early, therefore, in his plans for a preaching circuit in Galilee, he made his first move toward a permanent disciple band. Four of these who had been with him from the beginning, two sets of brothers and all fishermen, were well tested. Jesus was determined to invite them to share fully in his ministry. It was a crucial decision for the Lord.

An opportunity soon presented itself. His fame had spread so that crowds pressed about him eagerly when he spoke. Even early that morning when he appeared alone along the beach, he was instantly surrounded. The pressure of the throng backed him ever closer to the water's edge, so he stepped into a boat from which the men were away, washing the nets from the toil of the night just past. Knowing what he had in mind, it is not hard to suppose that it was no accident that he chose the craft owned by Simon Peter and his brother Andrew. He had surely seen that boat before. Docked alongside was the second, the property of Zebedee and sons, John and James. The men were partners in the fishing business (see Luke 5:1-11; Mark 1:16-20), and Jesus had his eye on the four of them.

He spoke from the vessel as his floating pulpit until he had finished his teaching. The four fishermen had returned and probably stood near the shoreline or sat together in the second fishing boat. He moved the craft to shore and asked Peter to take him out into the lake and cast their nets. In spite of the failure of the previous night's efforts, Simon obeyed the request. To the amazement of Peter and Andrew, the nets took a haul of fish the like of which the two veterans had never seen. Needing help, they made frantic signs to the Zebedee craft still at its mooring. The catch threatened to swamp both boats, and Peter knew that another evidence of the power of Jesus had accomplished it. It

was the right moment. As the two crafts headed shoreward together, he addressed all four, calling them to his cause. They
should leave their occupations and undertake his mission with
him. It could not have been too far from their minds. They had
for many months taken occasional leave of their toil at sea and
gone to join him in preaching and baptizing. It was not a far
leap of their faith to abandon the old way and enlist in his new
kingdom as fishers of men. They acted at once, ready to go
immediately. Indeed, Mark added the detail that John and James
left their father in the boat with the crew.

They were pressed into service almost at once. Jesus longed
to move about in the well-populated cities and towns of Galilee.
The urge to declare his gospel was strong within him. The Gospel
writers identify three evangelistic tours of Galilee during the next
year and a half. The first one was undertaken with the four new
disciples' going in each town into the synagogue. Preaching and
healing was the daily routine, and to Peter and the others miracles
became commonplace.[5] They would never entertain doubt that
their Master was sent from God or that he had authority over
creation and all its creatures, including mankind.

The time had come, however, for the circle to be enlarged.
The excitement grew as he progressed from town to town, and
his wondrous works brought yet more believers to his side. It
seems obvious that some of them joined him regularly, and it was
natural for him to become personally acquainted with them. He
would learn their names and perhaps permit them to assist his
four permanent attendants with the crowds. Above all, he must
have observed them carefully, asking questions which tested their
potential. He was ready to choose twelve men from among all
those who talked with him and to confer on them special status
and responsibility in establishing his kingdom.

It was a monumental decision. He was asking untrained and
obscure men to enter history, their names forever linked with

---

[5]Summaries of this first tour are recorded in Mark 1:36-39; Matthew 4:23-25.

Christianity. So urgently did he need the Father's counsel that
he spent all night in prayer (see Luke 6:12-16). At daybreak he
sent for all those who had identified with him, including the
four previously called to permanent duty. He had made his choices,
and there early in the morning he commissioned twelve of them
to a unique role in his kingdom. He named them apostles—"ones
sent" by special appointment to preach and minister the gifts
of the Messiah's realm.

There is no way to know the number of the others not chosen.
The Lord certainly had his reasons, and no objection was raised.
They were a diverse lot, all Galileans except one, Judas; and the
majority were fishermen. Seven of those selected had been previously mentioned in the Gospel narratives: the four disciples
already named, Philip and Nathanael,[6] and Matthew, who had
cast his lot with Jesus shortly before. The remaining five were
unknown to this point. Undoubtedly Jesus had found them by
the same insight which led to the other selections. A third set
of brothers was among the new appointees: James the son of
Alpheus and Judas (not Iscariot).[7] One political extremist appears
on the list, Simon the Zealot. The remaining two were Thomas,
a twin, and Judas the betrayer.

The next two and a half years, approximately, Jesus spent in
the company of these converts. They became his family. They
were by no means finished products. Often they seemed incapable
of comprehending Jesus' meanings. They stumbled over his parables, quarrelled among themselves, slept at their posts, sought
special position and advancement. Their Lord had to say to them
on more than one occasion, "O men of little faith." They tended
to be overprotective of Jesus, seeking to shield him from the press
of the sick, from involvement with those whom they called sinners,
and from the children who on occasions were placed in his arms.
One of them was prone to doubt; another denied with an oath

---

[6]Also known as Bartholomew. Men of the day often had two names.
[7]See Jude 1:1. He is also called Thaddeus.

that he knew him; one was lost by betrayal; and the rest except one deserted him during his trial and death. But Jesus understood them and loved them and gave himself to them. And after the brief defection at the cross, the eleven returned to his fellowship and rose to heights of courage and heroism which challenge all who would follow the Master.

THE TERMS OF THE KINGDOM

The apostles had no resource not available to contemporary disciples. They had their foibles and were subject to all the laws of the flesh. What changed them was that they kept company with Jesus! His call is still "Follow me"; the scheme has not been altered. By repentance and with faith one comes into a conscious relationship with Christ. There is a contract made to be a citizen of his kingdom, and it is openly declared. The further pledge is given to live by his teachings and to share the good news with others. These believers are committed to live under the rule of Jesus Christ while granting allegiance to their nation of birth or choice. This is the nature of the kingdom. This is the way to be saved! Salvation does not come by any act or intent of a man or woman. One is saved only by the person of Christ and by personal identity with him and is changed within by the same association that made new men of the disciples from Galilee. There is no alternative plan.

One wonders what might have been the outcome if on that first day Andrew and John had answered Jesus' question differently. He turned to inquire of them, "What do you seek?" The substance of the question was "What do you men want from me?" Suppose they had responded, "We want bread," or "Work a miracle to prove you are the Messiah," or "We don't really know; John the Baptist told us to follow." It is certain that Jesus would not have submitted to their terms. Since the sovereignty was his, he would manifest himself and accept followers only on *his* conditions, never on theirs. That rule has held true and is still in force.

Agreements with God are not negotiable on human terms.

The issues may be better seen in an analogy. The time has come, let us suppose, when the nation faces death pangs. Crisis has succeeded crisis until the political and social fabric is mortally torn. Old verities perish; landmark institutions crumble; chaos is in prospect. At the crucial moment a strong new leader arises and challenges, "Follow me and I will lead you out of this political morass and salvage our national pride." Where is the man or woman who would espouse his cause and join his banners without first determining the terms of that discipleship? Should not the obligations and risks be fully embraced? Further, would anyone accept the interpretations of his campaign manager *if* the man himself had spoken?

In a fashion quite as dramatic, as touching the way mankind is to be saved, Jesus the Messiah stood forth above the inadequacy of the law and summoned all the men of all the ages to God's radical experiment! The obligations were never hidden; nor were the conditions obscured. The adherents of the new kingdom were to bear his name, take the risks, and stake everything on the faith that an inner change in a person could accomplish what legislation and ritual had never never been able to achieve. Jesus called it "counting the cost." But again, as in the case of the human deliverer, if Jesus articulated the terms of discipleship beyond reasonable doubt, who is disposed to heed the lieutenants of religion? When the commander in chief has spoken, who dares modify his design for the realm he so proudly labeled as "my kingdom" and "my church"?

It has become quite the fashion, however, to relax the rigorous demands that creative discipleship imposes. Jesus makes no impossible assignments; he never asks of his converts more than they can give. Yet if his saving work is to change human nature so that no less an idea than being "born again" is adequate, then every believer must be in complete earnest about his or her response to the claims of Christ. There is no easy road to human regeneration, but Satan lures thousands down that same path to which he unsuccessfully tempted Jesus.

It is an affront to the Savior to deal in what some theologians have termed "cheap salvation." He paid a dear price for a gift which some handle cheaply. Whether by ignorance or evil intent, anyone who distorts the New Testament terms for salvation has taken on a fearful foe. To contest with Christ his authority on the way his sacrifice is to be operative is to stand in danger of a terrible judgment. In his plan, Jesus made no provision for the grace of God to be issued something on the order of fire or disaster insurance. The end of this popular offer from unnumbered pulpits is to "get to heaven" or have the "soul saved" quite apart from belonging to the kingdom. Jesus did not come to save souls; he came to save people—the whole person, the total personality! If "soul" is used as a synonym for "person," well and good; but if it refers to an invisible aura of feeling, a kind of pink glow which floats in the area of the breast, then it is but a subtle step to applying the claims of the cross to that same zone—and the individual thereby retains jurisdiction over the rest of the self. The net effect is that Christ has "saved" one component of personality, and the convert must be pled with unendingly to grudgingly yield other small segments to the lordship of Christ. This is often called consecration, but it is thought of as an optional second step. It was not so in the mind of the Master. He exempted no minute part of personality from his dominion.

Even the most sacred doctrine is not immune from such mishandling—the new birth. The event of birth normally progresses into the continuous life of the infant. No one ever dreams of separating the two. Birth is the indispensable entry into life, and life is the only possible reason for birth. Babies are not born for the sake of babies; each newborn begins immediately to become what was intended—a man or a woman. The life-principle is continuous. The Scriptures affirm that the Christian begins as a babe in Christ. There is no other way to enter eternal life. But there is not the slightest interruption in biblical doctrine between the birth from above and the continuing life in relation to the Lord of life. Membership in his kingdom is not an elective for those who want his salvation. To be born again means *to be born into* the kingdom of heaven! The Jesus who saves is the Jesus who reigns, and no choice is offered as to whether one prefers the one without the other.

Two specific issues regarding current ecclesiology demand attention to bring them into harmony with New Testament doctrine. Neither is wrong *per se*. Both have their dangers and are at times wrongly used. One is the matter of the church roll. Membership in a church has been so carelessly handled that it frequently challenges Jesus' definition of discipleship. To have one's name on the church roll is imputed to be a certificate of safety. It is a sort of visible edition of the "Lamb's book of life." To be in its listing has become, for many, an end in itself; and the mind is closed to further consideration of the saving appeal of Christ.

This is not on any authority of Scripture. The analogy there is not a roll; that is God's prerogative. He has his roll, but his church is designated as a "body." Members of the body are vitally related, not an inventory of parts—hands, ears, eyes, and so forth. One cannot, by definition, be a detached member of a body. The scandal of the enormous number of inactive and nonresident members is that if any of them should not be saved by their relation to the person of Jesus (and he only can ultimately judge), they have been insulated against the work of the Holy Spirit by their comfortable position. Their names are safely inscribed—in the church directory.

A case in point is not untypical. The weekly paper from a large and vigorous church contained the query, "Do you know where these folks are? We are trying to bring our membership rolls up to date." Then followed twenty-six names ranging in the alphabet only from *La* to *Le:*[8] "Mrs. Ellen Lacrue, A. C. Laing,

---

[8] Names changed for reasons of privacy.

Jr., John W. Laine, Frank A. Landes" . . . and on through the Landers and the Lankfords and the Langleys, eight people named Lee, down to David Lewiston. And the list will be continued the following week, and the next, and the next.

Where are the Lees and the LeDovanes and the Lemaisters? What were the circumstances of their claims to have joined themselves to Christ? Under what kind of invitation did they unite with his church? What would they say if one asked them whether they belong to the kingdom of God? No judgment can be made from without. The evidence is that some spokesman or agent for the gospel did not set forth adequately the terms of salvation as Jesus defined them.

This kind of compromise is related to a second issue—the aisle. The way onto the church roll is down the aisle. There is nothing mystical about "going forward." So far as can be known, Jesus did not make specific demands for any token signifying acceptance of the kingdom except baptism. In contemporary culture, as long as going to the front of a sanctuary to face the congregation signifies acceptance and commitment to the New Testament plan of salvation, then it is of course a valid invitation. But the way to be saved is not by extending the right hand. People are not redeemed by their experiences. They are redeemed by a person! They accept in experience; they accept by faith; they are able to accept through grace—but they are saved by the nature and the act of Jesus Christ!

ANOTHER KIND OF GOSPEL

It may very well be that certain modern styles of evangelism are perilously close to the errors which troubled the Galatian churches. Paul warned them against "a different gospel" (Gal. 1:6). Elements of Jewish legalism had altered some aspects of what the apostle had proclaimed to them. He implored them not to preach or believe any other kind of gospel except the one he brought as a minister of Christ. It would be equally heretical for anyone, under any motivation, to offer an alternate way to be saved! It seems certain that only a revival of sound biblical theology can stem the flood of church members who cannot be found and Christians who show no evidences of the disciplines of the kingdom of heaven.

Proclamation, popular style, can be measured only by its conformity to the standards of the Lord who founded his realm and set its requirements. Such conformation need not be a deterrent to popularity. Both the Baptist and Jesus were in high favor—as was the church while still in full flush after the endowment of the Holy Spirit (see Acts 2:46-47). The central issue is simply that of who sets the standard. The denominational consensus is not authoritative; the Scriptures are. Some preach repentance as a kind of emotional sorrow; the Bible speaks of bringing forth fruits worthy of repentance. People exhort others to "have faith"; Jesus urged, "Believe into me." [9] There is no Christian virtue in having faith in just anything. Faith must be had in Christ. Men may cry "Walk the aisle"; but Jesus said, "Follow me." Pulpits magnify the security of the saints; the Scriptures advocate the maturity of the saints. It is easy to glory in babes in Christ; the biblical goal is "men in Christ."

The net result of inept proclamation of New Testament fundamentals regarding salvation and the kingdom is that the average churchman does not comprehend the terms of discipleship. Largely by unprophetic preaching, people drift into the notion that they can have Christ's redemption in degrees—as little or as much as they wish. A dominant posture on doctrine has come to be "it seems to me." Had there been no objective events or a divine revelation, such subjective stance might be pardonable. But in the light of redemptive history and authoritative Scripture, primacy must be given to the way Jesus defined his kingdom and its requirements. God's plan for the ages is not up for ratification or referendum. He is simply not impressed with doctrinal positions

---

[9] This is the force of an invitation Jesus frequently offered.

of denominations or the views of those with strong leanings—in either direction.

Everything in the environment of the last quarter of the twentieth century militates against doctrinal integrity. It is an era of relativism, of the erosion of particularity. Sharp lines are unpopular. The tolerance demanded by society turns more to blandness. Compromise is the order of the day. The public handles Jesus as it does all other ideologies, and every man tends to be his own interpreter. A young man strolled aimlessly through the airport in Atlanta. His leather jacket was beautifully embroidered in colorful designs, obviously of Chinese style. The figure of a dragon curved around a legend which read: "Vietnam, 1972-1974 . . . . When I die I'm going to heaven; I've already been in hell." No one would take from him any credit due for duty as required by his country. But sympathy for his service does *not* include his right to determine how God will govern in the affairs assigned to the sovereignty of Christ the Savior! The keys of the kingdom have not been placed in the hands of the general public and its relative opinions.

It is no wonder that Jesus made a charge to his disciples which sounds strange at first hearing. Toward the end of the preaching career he warned them against the performance of the Mosaic law by the scribes and Pharisees. "They preach," he said, "but do not practice" (Matt. 23:3). Then he instructed them that they were not to be called *rabbi* (teacher), and James later repeated the injunction and broadened the application (see James 3:1). His admonition is pertinent in this era—"Let not many of you become teachers." There are often too many, at least of a type. Self-qualified teachers of religion are most evident on the youth scene, and a massive religious confusion is at least one inevitable result.

Up until the sixties the charge against the youth generation was its reluctance to speak of spiritual things. But the religious fads, succeeding one upon the other, have produced a totally different climate. Now opinions are easily held and loosely spoken.

Eastern cults are synthesized with Christian practices; mysticism and the occult color traditional faith; extremist groups on the fringe of the churches quickly find disciples. Contemporary young people have good feelings about Jesus of Nazareth, but they are bewildered. They need to have reliable teachers to interpret what Jesus commanded. Young and immature Christians have testimonies which are valid. Teaching ought to wait for understanding and testing in interpreting God's Word.

In the current religious mix, *discipline* is the lost word. It is not a favorite idea, human nature being what it is. Yet the role to which Jesus calls men and women is that of discipline—one who submits to his disciplines: in short, a learner! Christians are not born full-grown. Their initial experience does not fully inform them of all the claims of Jesus' kingdom. But they have enrolled in his school; they wear his baptismal uniform. There is no way to overemphasize or exhaust the biblical doctrines of the endless growth of everyone who has been born again. The Christian is not a saint, as the world sees saints; but he goes to school to Jesus Christ. That is why discipleship is not an impossible task. Perfection is not required, but learning is. No one need be free of error, but there is no exemption from the obligation to grow toward "the measure of the stature of the fullness of Christ." That is a part of the salvation in him, being full-grown.

A number of commentators have noted that the word of Jesus, "Take my yoke upon you" (Matt. 11:29), has probable meaning in a second direction, along with the obvious burden bearing. In a rabbinical sense, "to be yoked" meant to submit to a teacher. The student of Hillel, for instance, was said to wear his yoke—thus also the student of Jesus. The idea is strongly reinforced by the phrase "and learn from me." From the moment John and Andrew accepted him down to the profession of faith by the most recent convert, whoever believes in Jesus Christ becomes his disciple, his learner, in his kingdom. There is enough to learn to last a lifetime.

V
Need of a Physician
The Credentials of the King

*"Those who are well have no need of a physi-
cian, but those who are sick; I came not to call
the righteous, but sinners"* (Mark 2:17).

It was one of the scandals later assigned to Jesus—the kind
of people he attracted! He had already demonstrated by his choice
of the twelve the kind of folk who would comprise his kingdom.
They were common men, not ecclesiastics, and with no special
tutoring in the law. Their aptitude for the requirements of the
heavenly kingdom would come from inner sensitivity to the new
ways of God, never from endless disputations on the Mosaic law.
The twelve themselves were very unalike in temperament and
training, yet in Jesus' presence they were slowly transformed. At
the end they would be brothers in persecution and proclamation,
and the Zealot who was pledged to kill the traitor would sit
alongside the tax collector who had bought that favor from the
hated Romans and was thereby his enemy.

Jesus' early popularity brought together people of every sort,
of every class, and of every condition. There were the curious,
the mentally disturbed, the sick and crippled, the spies, soldiers,
public officials, anxious parents, those burdened by sin and guilt.
And, above all, where Jesus was there were the Pharisees and
Sadducees. Whatever the motive of the majority of the Master's
congregations, the reasons for the presence of these Jerusalemites
is unquestioned. The Pharisees[1] were the rigid legalists and purists
concerning the law and particularly the traditions of Israel. The
Sadducees controlled the priesthood and the enforcement of the

---

[1]The word means Separatist. Their zealous patriotism had turned them into
bigots. They were very influential, but never very numerous. Josephus indicates
that there were no more than six to seven thousand.

legal codes. The more the popular excitement rose, even in Galilee, the more the religious leaders feared and despised Jesus. Unable to deny his marvelous words and works, they blindly intensified their hatred. They were there to ensnare him and gather evidence against him.

It was to these men of closed and bitter heart that Jesus made his significant remark, "I came not to call the righteous, but sinners." Having no sense of need, confessing no sin, they thought themselves righteous. As well men have no need of the physician, these religionists held themselves aloof from his ministries. Admitted sinners might need his saving grace, but not they. Common people could embrace Jesus' kingdom; the Pharisees were irrevocably committed to the heritage from Moses and the fathers.

THE ISSUES OF THE KINGDOM

To this diverse host of men and women Jesus laid out the dimensions of his kingdom. He did not travel about aimlessly seeing what good he could accomplish; he taught and healed always with but one end in view. That he succeeded in establishing the design of his reign and his concept of God's purpose is evident from the increasing surveillance and hostility of the religious rulers from Jerusalem.

At issue was *Jesus' claim that he was sent from God.* The Pharisees thought themselves, along with their scribes, to be authoritative as touching the law and prophets. They well knew that the Messiah would come, but the man of Galilee in no way fitted their picture of God's anointed. They had become convinced that when the Christbb[2] arrived he would come from the ecclesiastical hierarchy, not from an obscure Galilean village. They would have asked in derision the question Nathanael spoke only in surprise, "Can anything good come out of Nazareth?" (John 1:46). They had concluded that he would make a regal entry into his

---

[2] "Christ" is the Greek word which means the same thing as the Hebrew term "Messiah"—the sent one, the anointed one.

domain, and certainly warlike qualities would be demanded to deliver Israel from the Roman captor. Messiah would appear dramatically, cataclysmically, and sign and portent would accompany his manifestation.

Moreover, the people Jesus associated with were beneath their contempt. Haughty and class-conscious, the Pharisees kept aloof from the very ones with whom the Teacher surrounded himself. The sick and demented whom he healed acclaimed him; women who had been restored adored him; but the religious rulers despised him. They had no time for the children he held on his lap. Above all, he associated and ate with "sinners," and for this latter group the Pharisees held a special scorn. Chief spot in their hostility was reserved for publicans—the Jewish tax collectors who had collaborated with the Romans and garnered Caesar's levies to support the very forces which occupied their homeland. One of Jesus' disciples who stood by, probably taking notes on his Master's teachings, was himself such a "turncoat" and thereby an offense to them. His name was Matthew.[3]

Incidents such as the conversion of Zacchaeus further served to enrage the proud Pharisees. This man was not only a publican; he was a chief official in the Roman revenue service and had prospered from his ill-gotten gain. Something the Master had said somewhere intrigued him, and he made it possible to encounter Jesus in an unlikely place. Jesus stopped under the tree in which the man of small stature was perched on the lower branches and smilingly announced, "Zacchaeus, make haste and come down; for I must stay at your house today" (Luke 19:5). It was undoubtedly a happy visit, and a thoroughly changed Zacchaeus tacitly admitted that he had defrauded his fellow citizens. Such behavior convinced the Pharisees that Jesus could not possibly have been Israel's Savior!

The Pharisaic view of sinners stood in sharp contrast with Jesus' position. They were relentless in condemnation; he had come to

[3] See Luke 5:27. Matthew's other name was Levi. See also Matthew 9:9.

change them at the core and make them into his family of the redeemed. Those who had turned to him for salvation had been forgiven much and loved much,[4] and their new attitude made them fit material for the daring good news to be sent into all the earth. There is nothing new about judgment, but a chance to be forgiven and restored is the most welcome tiding ever told. And there is an inexhaustible supply of sinners awaiting the news. Yet the powerful religionists obstructed him at every turn and in the name of God. When he performed undeniable acts, in their frustration they attributed his powers to a league with Satan. When he spoke great wisdom, they demanded a sign of his authority. When he presumed to teach them, they distorted his answers and tried to ensnare him with words. His truth, so far as their hearing was concerned, always fell on stony ground.

A second issue was raised by the Pharisees in *their constant accusation that Jesus set aside the Mosaic law*. This became the focal point of their attacks, and ultimately such charges would be central in their witness against him at his trials. They could not tolerate his challenge to the Jewish establishment of religion. A particular target was Jesus' conduct on the sabbath. Jesus observed the sabbath, but as God ordained it, not as the scribes and scholars had embroidered it beyond recognition. In his kind of kingdom Jesus would never allow any institution or regulation to take precedence over the individual. It would be the spirit of the law that would motivate his disciples, not bare-boned codes which demanded rote obedience and usually managed to enslave.

The sabbath controversy was joined at the beginning of the Galilean preaching tour. Accompanied by his disciples, he was making his way to an unknown destination by way of a route that led through a field of wheat or barley. The grain was ripe and the men were hungry, so they plucked the heads from the stalk and rubbed them in their hands to separate the kernels from the chaff—but it was the sabbath day. The Pharisees leaped to

---

[4]These are Jesus' words. Read the winsome story in Luke 7:36-50.

the attack. The act of preparing the barley for eating was thresh-
ing, they said, and such labor was in violation of their rules.

It would have been fruitless at this early stage for Jesus to
have reasoned with his critics on the basis of his own understanding
of God's purpose for a day of rest. So he resorted to their style
of argument and cited how David himself had caused his men
to eat of the dedicated bread in the tabernacle. Special loaves
were baked by the priests under elaborate prescriptions, and the
bread was presented to God. It was called "bread of the Presence"
(Mark 2:26). After the week, and when the fresh loaves were
ready, the old bread was placed on a special table in the sanctuary
area and was eaten by the priests during the performance of their
duties. David was not of the priesthood and was not eligible to
eat this food, but under the pressure of need he did so. The Jews
would find no fault with their hero-king, but Jesus affirmed that
a man greater than David had come on the scene. He said boldly
of himself that he was "lord even of the sabbath" (Mark 2:28).

The matter was of such consequence to Jesus that he aggressively
pursued this controversial issue. It was not a time for caution.
His opponents were undoubtedly incensed by his unheard-of
claim—that he was equal to the Father in his own lordship over
the sabbath. The news traveled fast; and soon afterward, on what
possibly was the next holy day, the Pharisees were present, having
formed themselves into an investigative committee. As the people
were gathered in the synagogue, they found an occasion to force
Jesus to restate his position or to back down. A man was there
whose hand [5] was useless, probably as the result of injury. They
confronted Jesus with a question. Pointing to the man, they asked,
"Is it lawful to heal on the sabbath?" (Matt. 12:10). They were
daring him to violate their own doctrine that illness or injury
was God's just punishment for sin and was, therefore, his will.

---

[5] Note that *Dr.* Luke, as he often did, made a more complete diagnosis of
the condition than the other writers. He observed that it was the man's *right*
hand (Luke 6:6).

Jesus accepted the challenge. Boldly he requested the injured man to step out before them all and defied the hypocritical pietists by countering with a question of his own. Would they rescue a sheep from a pit if it were the only one they had? Mark's word that "they were silent" (Mark 3:4) indicates a sullen embarrassment which turned to rage when Jesus told the man to stretch out the hand—and it was restored whole before their eyes. Mark commented further that Jesus looked at the Pharisees with anger. This is precisely the way God would act when men, in his name, placed regulation and rigid religious forms in a rank superior to the needs of humanity. Anger is a moral reaction against wrong. But at the same time, the author says that Jesus was grieved. These were twin responses to men who had made their hearts like stone against his truth. The men and women of Jesus' kingdom would have altogether another view on what should be done on the sabbath.

He would not abolish the established day which God decreed, but he did have the right to fulfill the Father's intent. He was not the slave of a sacred time period, and neither would his followers be. He interpreted the law; he would fill it with new meaning and, by his resurrection, even give it a new name. Those who in the future claimed his name would please God far more by their proclamation that "He is risen" than those who conformed to meticulous rules and ridiculous restrictions. These were not the commandments of God. "Observe the sabbath day," he had said, "to keep it holy"; and he had prohibited work so that his people might rest. Scribal tradition had so distorted the holy day that it became a burden of magnitude; Israel was in bondage to the Pharisaic adornment of God's law. It is safe to assume that not many statements by Jesus rankled in their legalistic minds with the intensity of his word that "the sabbath was made for man, not man for the sabbath." If Jesus' kingdom was going to take that kind of turn, then it had made implacable foes of all who had vested interests in maintaining traditional Judaism.

A third struggle arose over *the fashion by which Jesus flaunted scribal tradition.* These petty regulations did not have the force of law as had been true of the commandments God gave through Moses. They were, rather, the outgrowths of centuries of usage and custom which came from the teaching and transmission of the Jewish legal system. The scribes had "interpreted" the spirit of the law beyond recognition.

Tradition was the proper word for such practices, as is made clear in the debate over the disciples who ate with "unwashed" hands (Mark 7:1-9). Clean hands may be desirable before a meal, but the scribal restriction was not at the point of sanitation. Their concern was ceremonial defilement. After mixing with other people, an elaborate ritual was prescribed to restore the individual to the rank of the ceremonially clean. This could, if water were not available, be done by rubbing the hand and arm with the other hand tightly clenched. The Greek word for the act actually means "fist." Only then were the strict Jews free to eat. This was by no command of God; it was manifestly the tradition of the elders.

But Jesus' men did not submit to such a shallow definition of the religion of Jehovah. The Master always went to the heart of things, to the spirit of the law. Evil, Jesus would teach them, came from inner dispositions, not external contamination of hands or vessels or the like. So when he was reprimanded on so shallow a cause, his retort was a classic statement. He summed up their preoccupation with slight offenses in withering irony: "You have a fine way of rejecting the commandment of God, in order to keep your tradition" (Mark 7:9). It is an eternal judgment against any religion of form and ceremony!

Jesus also resisted this type of dealing with God's commandments when the same foes charged him with not requiring his disciples to fast (Mark 2:18). Abstaining from food had been an instruction to Israel from the beginning for the Day of Atonement. It was likewise practiced, both individually and corporately, as an expression of grief or of an earnest desire in seeking God and as a token of the people humbling themselves. The later prophets chided the Jews who implied that an act of denial in itself was pleasing to God. Indeed, they stated that without right attitudes, fasting was vain (see Isa. 58:3-8; Jer. 14:12).

The Lord himself did not practice this discipline except under great spiritual stress, as during his wilderness temptation; and then the motive came from within. There is no evidence that he gave his disciples any such regimen as a rule of the kingdom. He presumed that they would fast, but warned them to examine carefully the spirit of the deed (see Matt. 6:16-18). But the strict Pharisees placed great importance on this ritualistic observance, fasting on Mondays and Thursdays (see Luke 18:11-12). Against such a background the fasting controversy arose.

The situation likely resulted from an event which had rankled the Pharisees and their scribes, which occurred just after Matthew, the tax collector, had been summoned to follow Jesus. As an act of appreciation, Matthew had prepared a great feast (Luke 5:29); and Jesus sat at the table in the publican's house along with a host of others who gathered Caesar's tribute. That was enough to infuriate the Jews. But the happening was complicated by the likelihood that the banquet fell on one of the rigorous fasting days. So while the Pharisees grudgingly denied themselves food, Jesus and his friends were making merry. That was too much for them: Jesus not only ate with sinners, but he went against one of their tests of piety.

The Master's response to their criticism presents another facet of his kingdom and the conduct of its citizens. It introduces the bright note of joy and celebration! He likened the mood of the Christian in fellowship with his Lord to the eagerness and joy of wedding guests. Communing with God is not a time for mourning. Such times of grief may very well come later, but their existence will depend on the situation. The people of God learn to act with appropriateness, rejoicing with those who rejoice and

weeping with those who weep. The Christian faith is not always
a state of unadulterated bliss. Indeed, the Christian has the burdens
and cares of all humanity, plus the compassion of God for others.
But the kingdom men and women also have the warm presence
of their Lord, who is their friend. There is joy in their salvation,
and that is the spirit in which the burdened world is to be invited
to the table where God communes with his new kind of people.

The fourth confrontation between Jesus and the religionists of
his day was on *the issue of the definition of God's kingdom*. The
Jerusalem doctors of the law had entertained no idea but that
they were in complete charge of the divine plan, which had forever
been committed to the chosen people. They foresaw no contin-
gency which would take the reins out of their hands. The age-old
covenant was in force, as they saw it; and they fully intended
to maintain it. They had the law and the right to interpret it
on their side.

From the time of the preaching of John the Baptist, they had
been first vaguely disturbed and then moved to violent concern
at the turn of events in Judea and Galilee. The people were
listening to the heretical teaching along the Jordan and throughout
Galilee. Even in Jerusalem, the appearance of the Nazarene caused
a sensation, and certain influential people had been won over
to the new cause. It was for this reason that they would frequently
question Jesus and would increase disputes with him both in tempo
and intensity. It was manifestly impossible for the kingdom of
God to go both ways. If Jesus' way prevailed, then their position
was untenable. They saw that clearly.

But that battle was one that Jesus was geared for, and to
precipitate that discussion was to play into his hands. The basic
thesis of his message was that God was now fulfilling the old
regime of law and ushering in a totally new kind of rule. The
kingdom of heaven would not be an alteration or refurbishing
of the old covenant; it would be an entirely new concept. The
law, the Temple, the priestly sacrificial system—everything—

would undergo drastic change. Whatever the old contract between God and man had intended would be accomplished in a new and better way. But the outward was to become inward and the ritualistic to become spiritual. God had intended this transformation from the first, and the time had come!

Within the scope of brief twin parables (see Luke 5:36-39) Jesus drew the issues sharply. His memory turned, perhaps, to an unfortunate experience his mother had had in his boyhood. She attempted to patch a well-worn garment with a piece of new cloth. It did well until the clothing had to be washed, but then the shrinkage of the new patch pulled the old tear and made it worse. Everyone understood the significance of that. Judaism had served its purpose, and done it well. It had taken a minority race of no power or prestige and made it the world's greatest teacher of religion. Priest and prophet had prepared a people for God's use, but the form had gone as far as it could go. In its present hands it had become threadbare tradition. The leaders thought the system itself was final, but it was neither sacred nor eternal; therefore, the mold had to be discarded for the realization of the larger, fuller truth. Judaism could not be renovated, patched up; it was time for a new design.

The accompanying parable was not repetitive, but supplementary. Jesus appealed to the same common fund of experience: new wine vigorously fermenting in an old and hardened skin will rupture the wineskin and spill the wine. The wine is the significant element, not the bottle. The person and message of Jesus Christ causes change, but his truth is harmonious with the past manifestation of God. It was to be transmitted from ancient generations to the new in perishable vessels and not spilled. The central point now is to conserve the continuous and progressive revelation of God to man. But the heady wine of the gospel burst the Judaistic wineskins. It stretched the old bottles beyond limits. It was time for a new kind of righteousness. Jesus would have nothing to do, then or now, with any self-righteous Society for the Veneration and Preservation of Old Wineskins!

THE SIGNS OF THE KINGDOM

More, however, than the conflict in doctrine and definition, the aspect of Jesus' work which raised excitement to fever pitch and sent the Jewish rulers into paroxysms of rage was his healing miracles. Their history abounded in narratives of God's mighty works with Israel, but the recent centuries had seen no evidence that God was ready to act in their behalf as he once did. Yet when Jesus began to perform wondrous works the reaction of his influential detractors was cynicism. Undoubtedly, they said, it was a diabolical plot; and the Galilean must be in league with Beelzebub, the prince of devils.

Strangely enough, this hostility of the Pharisees and Sadducees represents the first occasion in the Bible record on which anyone had a problem with miracles. They had always been regarded as typical acts of God. One reason was that the politico-religious structure of the New Testament period furnished the climate for the emergence of philosophical thought. Old Testament men had proceeded on the assumption that all knowledge was from God; they had received truth by revelation, not reason. It was the advent of philosophy, and later science, which gave knowledge its humanistic character—that is, the achievement of truth by the unaided power of the human mind. The Jews had come into close contact with Greek culture and thought and had learned something of the world they lived in. They then began to make observations about the nature of things, generalized on such evidence, and drew certain conclusions. Those concepts they accepted as fact.

This process had happened specifically in the Hebrew religious setting in the matter of disease and human suffering. Jesus' contemporaries attributed all illness, as they did every other event, to the will of God. Disease, as they had observed it, was the unquestioned result of sin; and the consequences were all in God's scheme of things (see John 9:2). Whoever, therefore, undertook to heal the body was acting in contradiction to the divine will. Healing arts were heartily disapproved and condemned.

A certain reinforcement of this position of Jewish leadership was found in the practices of the pagan world of Greek and Roman. Healing was known in the Mediterranean world and was chiefly associated with religion. Aesculapius was the patron divinity to whom petitions were made. His temples were the only hospitals of the ancient world, and his shrines were dedicated to his curative touch. Even so, the gods of the pantheon were thought to be concerned only with the healthy. The sick and deformed were largely left to their fate. The doctors of law in Jerusalem could not miss the point that it was around these outcasts that the miracles of Jesus clustered.

As the scientific era progressed, it lured thinkers along a false path that led them to conclude that there were no spiritual powers in the universe relevant to healing except those which yield to scientific research. By so doing a formidable foe arose which remains a stumbling block to understanding miracles. It was the definition, almost universally held, that a miracle is a *violation of the laws of nature*. So long as this is assumed to be fact, then in an orderly universe there would indeed be a presumption against miracles.

"Nature" is a concept which is not well defined in the Scriptures. It belongs more to later Greek thought, when the world was accepted as secular and operated by immutable laws. Indeed, in the Old Testament there is no Hebrew word for *nature*. The creation was always attributed to God and was often the subject of praise (see Pss. 8:3; 19:1-6; 65:6-13; Amos 4:13). In the view of the writers, the handiwork of God never lost its miraculous character. Throughout the Bible this mood prevails;[6] and it is clear that if one believes in the God who created the universe, sustains it, and controls it, then most of the difficulties with

---

[6] In the New Testament the use of the term *nature* is encountered, but usually in casual references. See Romans 2:14; 11:24; 1 Corinthians 11:14.

miracles have thereby been dealt with.

The architect of the later philosophical position that *miracle* must be defined as a contradiction of natural law is Benedict Spinoza, 1632-1677. Most subsequent skeptical views have been variations of the position of this Dutch philosopher of rationalism. Yet scientists have become much less confident that nature's laws are absolute. Change still goes on. Indeed, Augustine, over a thousand years before Spinoza, had declared that miracles were not violations of nature, since nature was nothing but the will of God concerning any particular object. It was in error, he said, to say that a portent was contrary to the natural order, since it occurred according to the will of God.

It may safely be assumed, then, that in establishing his kingdom Jesus would never have contemplated the suspension of the laws of the universe! That is a discredited theory. The Lord who created the natural order (see John 1:3) at no time interrupted the reign of law. He worked with the Father, never in contradiction to him. Thus a far more apt definition of the Master's "signs and wonders" needs to be employed.

Such definition is best sought by examining the purpose of Jesus for his new reign. He was fulfilling God's eternal plan at which the Almighty had been ceaselessly at work. In the incarnation Jesus broke through into the human situation from that high spiritual realm where he lived in unique relationship with the Father. It was natural that he should bring with him the energies of that plane of existence. These would not be out of harmony with the physical world since God was the author of all life. So miracles to heal and bless mankind were the signs of the new age, the new order which Christ inaugurated. They heralded a new era of spiritual power and a spiritual plane of being.

A miracle, then, can be defined as an event under the reign of law, natural or supernatural, in which one sees a revelation of God and through which the miracle-worker accomplishes his redeeming purposes by the release of energies from a higher plane than that which one ordinarily experiences. Such events were clearly indicated for Jesus as he set up his kingdom. He had come to save; and he asserted his right to heal all of life, spiritual or physical, as befitted his own design. It was never his act or intent to breach the cosmic order; he conformed always to the law of the higher plane he came to manifest. Yet from the earthbound viewpoint of ordinary people, Jesus appeared to set aside the scheme of nature. In point of fact he only acted normally for one who lived at his level of experience. His miracles were only the operation of his higher law of love.

Variation is allowable in a dynamic universe in which God dwells. It is not caprice because God is law-abiding. But he will express himself for loving ends. Perhaps this truth can be best seen by an analogy. The toddler at two has been thoroughly taught the routines of his family. The lad has learned by endless repetition what to expect when he awakes in the morning. The sights and sounds and smells of his small world of home are dependable, invariable. There is always the orange juice, the breakfast, the bath. He knows what to expect. He cannot have sweets because it's too early; he cannot have Mother's undivided attention because she must attend to her work; Daddy has already gone to the office. Schedules prevail; the household is subject to normalcy.

But one morning he awakes—and things are different. Both parents are watching him expectantly. He is bundled into a robe and taken straightway to the family room where a lustrous and shining tree dazzles him. Underneath its festive lights is an assortment of books and toys which amazes and delights him. Juice is served as he sits exploring the treasure he has discovered; bath and breakfast routines are set aside; he is tempted with sweets which ordinarily are denied; he is made to pose for pictures; his own slightest wish is granted. Even Dad is home and shows no sign of going to work.

The boy has experienced the first Christmas that he remembered. Could it always be this way? He might devoutly wish so;

but no, old patterns would return, for they are best. His mother and father had only interrupted daily schedules because there were realities in his world of which he was not yet aware. Loving parents were not reluctant to let usual procedures be superceded for the moment so that other values might be known to their son. It was fitting that they should express themselves, even though it was on another plane than the one to which the child was accustomed.

When one considers that Christ was not a prisoner in his own universe, the economy of miracles in his ministry is remarkable. Clearly he did not wish to be known as a "miracle man"; he had resisted that use of sensation in the wilderness temptation. He employed miracles sparingly, and only to serve his essential mission. He did not heal to demonstrate his power or to overawe the people and compel belief. He had a single motive—it was to act out his loving nature and character as he revealed himself as the saving One! He reacted normally, as God would, to hurt and sin; he healed and forgave and restored; and when all failed, he wept.

One can visualize a Christian physician visiting in a remote region of Asia or Africa. He is invited into a village where he is hospitably received, yet he is distressed at the sight of children having a poultice of mud and herbs applied by a witch doctor to serious infections. He knows that such primitive treatment sometimes works, but he cannot lay aside his scientific knowledge and training or his deep longing to make people well. So he asks for the right to examine the children, cleans the lesions, and applies the penicillin he carries with him. The rapid recovery of the patients may seem to be a miracle to the fearful parents, but to the doctor it was only the application of medical science which he practiced regularly. He was not trying to startle or impress them to constrain them to listen when he spoke, or to persuade them that his civilization was better than theirs. He was merely manifesting his own character.

Authority to Heal and Forgive

When Jesus performed deeds of healing he did so because he *was* the Great Physician and was only acting in conformity to his nature. He had the authority and used it. The notion of *authority* played an important part in his dealings with the Jews. The people recognized at once that he did not teach them in the same manner as the scribes. Instead of voluminous quotation of opinions of others, the Master asserted the right to speak truth from his own competence, "as one who had authority" (Mark 1:22). The Greek word used is *exousia*, which means literally "from out of one's being." The priests and elders were troubled by his unauthorized presumption to be a rabbi. They asked him pointedly, "By what authority are you doing these things?" (Mark 11:28). In his own mind Jesus required no human certification; he carried his own credentials: "But I say unto you."

Early in the Galilean ministry he faced the issue of his authority. He had come to Capernaum and was "at home" (Mark 2:1), very likely the house of Simon Peter. Since he would frequently be in residence there, it has been logically supposed by some that Peter would have made some preparation for the inevitable crowds. It may be that the small open courtyard of the house had been temporarily covered over by laths and loose tiles. In this central area Jesus stood, and the people looked out from all the surrounding rooms, while the crowd spilled over into the street.

To this site came four men bearing on a pallet a young paralytic, probably a relative. Finding no way to get through the press of people, the enterprising four would not be outdone; so they took their charge up the outside stairs to the low, flat roof. Knowing where Jesus was located, they were determined to lower the stretcher by ropes right before him. It would be a simple matter to uncover the roof and do no damage to the house as they would if permanent tiles had been set in plaster and reinforced with stone.

It is a unique scene to visualize as Jesus saw the pallet lowered and looked up into the four expectant faces above him. He responded warmly to the situation and shocked the assembly by saying, "My son, your sins are forgiven." There was no word about his legs but about his sins. It is difficult not to conclude that the paralysis and his sin were related. Jesus had spiritual energies which have powerful effect on the body, and enough is known about functional ailments caused by guilt so that the possibility cannot be discounted. So the curative factor might have been the authoritative word from the Master that he was released from the guilt which had alienated him from God and brought on his condition.

The words "forgive sin" sent a shock wave through the assemblage, and they correctly judged that by his action Jesus claimed to be God. Forgiveness was God's specialty; speaking the word of healing to the lame man was the sign visibly given that he had the authority to forgive. It was his gracious summons to all sinners, whether physically diseased or not, to enter his world which he called the kingdom of heaven and to use the new energies available to them.

From this and other miracles a common aspect is seen—the matter of faith as the necessary environment for Christ's mighty works. In the case of the paralytic, all the writers stipulate that the primary reason for Jesus' cure was "And when Jesus saw their faith" (Mark 2:5)—the faith of the four *and* the patient. The atmosphere created by belief is an aid to further belief, and faith tends to falter if it stands too long alone. The man on the stretcher took heart from the expectancy of those who believed in the possibility of his healing, and it was easier to respond to the confidence he heard in Jesus' voice. Indeed, Jesus once affirmed that he did few mighty works in Nazareth "because of their unbelief" (Matt. 13:58).

The same factor of faith is decisive as he "went about doing good." The daughter of a high-ranking synagogue official was critically ill (see Mark 5:21-43). Her father's faith was sufficient to bring Jesus to his house. Once there, alone in the silent room with only his closest companions, he spoke the words of life and health to the child. On the way to her bedside he had been touched by an infirm woman who believed that she could claim his power by her touch. What was the reward of those who by faith acknowledged they had need of a physician? One answer was typical of them all: "Your faith has made you well." The energies of the kingdom flow along the route of faith.

In every case Christ's works conformed to his purpose to manifest the advantages and the terms of his new reign. Every miraculous event served to reveal God in his redeeming role. This use of his healing energies seemed to Jesus to be an appropriate announcement of his kingdom. When he sent the apostles on a circuit of Galilee, divided into teams of two, his instructions were: "Preach as you go, saying, 'The kingdom of heaven is at hand.' Heal the sick, raise the dead, cleanse lepers, cast out demons" (Matt. 10:7-8).

Moreover he himself submitted to a self-imposed test as to whether or not the new order had arrived. In an hour when the faith of the now-imprisoned John the Baptist burned low, the Forerunner sent a famous message to Jesus. He asked, "Are you he who is to come, or shall we look for another?" (Luke 7:19-23). Had the baptizer's hopes been too high, or had the messianic kingdom actually come? As a reply, Jesus "cured many," and then pointed to these cures as the evidence that the kingdom was in force: the blind received sight; lame men walked; the deaf heard; lepers were made clean; and the poor were given the gospel. It was expected behavior for the Messiah-King.

For those who had eyes to see, it was also a completion of prophecy. Long before Isaiah had foreseen the Day of the Lord and had spoken of it in terms which Jesus fulfilled.

> *"Then the eyes of the blind shall be opened,*
>   *and the ears of the deaf unstopped;*
> *then shall the lame man leap like a hart,*
>   *and the tongue of the dumb sing for joy.*
> *For waters shall break forth in the wilderness,*
>   *and streams in the desert."* (Isa. 35:5-6)

VI
The Violent Kingdom
The Mysteries of the Kingdom

> *"The law and prophets were until John; since
> then the good news of the kingdom of God is
> preached, and every one enters it violently."*
>
> *(Luke 16:16)*

Listening to Jesus was never dull. Not only was his fresh content of teaching startling, but his mode of expression produced wonderment as well. His approach was novel; he used exaggerated figures of speech; his parables were often puzzling; and his applications were boldly shocking. Mark had a favorite term for the people's reactions which the disciples so often observed. "They were astonished." [1] The word *astonished* itself means struck by a blow. Jesus' words frequently had that impact.

The net result was that one had to listen to him carefully in order to know what was said—and what he meant by what he said. Such requirements are still in force. They are in keeping with the nature of his new kingdom. God no longer deals with his people in obvious demonstrations of might. His communication is not from a mountain quaking at his majesty, but in the "still, small voice" heard by the perceptive. It is the difference between the disciplines in childhood versus maturity: one is explicit, even noisy; the other subtle and suggestive. It is the reason Jesus so often warned his hearers that they had to have "ears that hear" and "eyes that see," else the truth would elude them. No one has captured this concept better than Phillips Brooks in the text of perhaps the finest hymn of the Messiah's coming.

> How silently, how silently,
>   The wondrous gift is given!
> So God imparts to human hearts
>   The blessings of His heaven.

---

[1] Examples may be seen in Mark 1:22; 6:2; 7:37; 10:26.

> No ear may hear His coming,
>   But in this world of sin,
> Where meek souls will receive him still,
>   The dear Christ enters in.[2]

This kind of sensitivity is required for kingdom citizens if they would catch the overtones of Jesus' enigmatic phrase concerning his realm, "every one enters it violently." It is the second time he used such words (see Matt. 11:12), and they appear to present yet another contrast between the dominion of law and the new age ushered in by John the Baptist. Under the covenant with Israel, no subtlety was needed to ascertain who was included or what was expected of them. That regimen, at least in the manner it had been practiced, produced a dullness of spirit which prevented perception of what God was doing before their eyes. The leaders of religion, therefore, stood passively mouthing their platitudes while publicans and sinners rushed past them into the kingdom. Jesus had opened the floodgates of redemption, and both he and the baptizer had implored the sons and daughters of Israel to the enthusiasm and fire required to participate in it. Jesus pled for moral earnestness and spiritual passion, for taking risks, for counting no cost too great.[3] This was the violent pursuit to which he exhorted them. Yet, Jesus concluded, should they wonder if by his gracious invitation to all humanity he thereby destroyed the law? His answer was clear. No, he did not set aside God's law; every minute part of it would be conserved and fulfilled in the new covenant with mankind.

Everything in Jesus' preaching was harmonious with his appeal to adventure and fervor. He admired energy. The characters he employed in teaching were never sitting in contemplation; they were active and forceful. He spoke of fishermen straining at bursting nets, builders at their trade, armies on the move, laborers in the vineyard, sowers and harvesters in the fields, jewel mer-

---

[2] "O Little Town of Bethlehem," stanza three.
[3] See the strong language he used in Luke 9:59-62; 13:24; 14:26.

chants searching, investors earning profit, stewards at their masters' bidding, and shepherds seeking lost sheep.

Moreover, he scorned moral neutrality and harmlessness. In parables he applauded forceful action. The priest and Levite did no harm to the man who "fell among thieves"; but they did no good either, and for that Jesus condemned them. The fig tree was cursed not because it bore stinking figs, but because it produced none at all. The five foolish bridesmaids did not extinguish their lamps by misusing them; they were guilty by reason of apathy and neglect. The unfaithful steward expected to be lauded by his master because he had not misused his funds, but found himself rejected because he made *no* use of them. Those who found themselves in condemnation in the judgment scene were startled to the point of protest. They had never taken another's food or water or clothing; nor had they unjustly imprisoned anyone. They were harmless and expected to be rewarded for it. The Lord's wrath still burns through this shallow concept of virtue as he cried, "As you did it not to one of the least of these, you did it not to me" (Matt. 25:45).

The Secrets of the Kingdom

It is obvious, then, that the concept of kingdom put forth by Jesus stood in sharp contrast to the expectancy of the Jews taught by generations of scribes and Pharisees. So strange was it that the Lord told his disciples plainly that they would have to penetrate deeper levels of truth: "To you has been given the secret of the kingdom of God" (Mark 4:11). But his purpose was not to produce an exclusive religious society; rather, it was to select a circle of those who understood the nature of his kingdom and could themselves become teachers, who would admit others. All are invited, but there is a stringent requirement: "Unless one is born anew, he cannot see the kingdom of God" (John 3:3). It takes a new nature to perceive a new realm.

This gracious inclusiveness is made clear throughout the New

Testament, where the word *mystery* refers not to secrets known only to the elite, but to things once hidden but now revealed.[4] God is going to make himself known, and he enlists the citizens of his kingdom "as servants of Christ and stewards of the mysteries of God" (1 Cor. 4:1). It is for this reason that disciples are "learners," keeping company with their Lord and growing in their knowledge of the nature of his rule. They need to be specialists in fulfillment, else they will not make the transition from the manifest terms of the old covenant to the mysteries of the new.

There is a perceptible difference between the government of God under the law and after Christ. In each case God is at the center; but in the Old Testament the center was vague, indistinct. People knew God but dimly. Even Abraham and Moses groped in the early, misty stages of revelation for his name and his purposes. But the circumference of rule and regulation which surrounded Israel was discernable, conspicuous. The requirements were plain; the boundaries marked; the commandments vivid. Indeed, it was precisely because they knew their God so inadequately that their limitations were so well drawn. It was the elementary stage; the law was the tutor to bring them toward maturity—ultimately to Christ, the Teacher.

In the new Testament there is a dramatic reversal. In Jesus God was fully revealed. The center is now clear; the Father is known to his children. Consequently the circumference of behavior and application is indistinct, ill defined. No one need prescribe for Christians what they cannot do on the Lord's Day or which part of their living must be tithed. It is no longer required that they bind themselves with an oath, or pray at stated intervals, or make offerings of thanksgiving on schedule. The conduct and devotion the Lord wants from his people they will give because they are vitally related to the person at the center. There are rules, but the rules are derived from the relationship.

---

[4] Paul speaks to this definition in Ephesians 3:3,4,9.

THE KINGDOM COME NEAR

It was Jesus' central task, then, to instruct the largest possible segment of the population as to the radically new dominion over which he was Lord. For the twelve it was an intensive training mission. They, above all, should comprehend these elements in religion never before advocated. The taught would then become teachers. Jesus could have established a school and trained likely candidates; but he chose, rather, to take the issues to the people. He had confidence in his message, and he did not hesitate to expose his distinctive truths to the masses. Thus is explained the importance of the traveling phase of his ministry.

The long and fruitful two years of uninterrupted teaching in Galilee, the territory surrounding it, and in Judea became the heart of Jesus' work. It was there that he carefully prepared the foundations for his unique kingdom. He presented himself and the blueprint of his messianic reign to the people, along with its privileges and requirements. During this period he developed the parable as his chief teaching tool, using it to illustrate his new standard of righteousness. But the painstaking training of the twelve was never far from the center of his attention.

Spending the bulk of the time in Galilee was warranted by the large population of the province. Josephus the historian states that there were three thousand cities and towns in the region— probably an exaggerated claim, but it reflects the density with which Galilee was peopled. It is not hard to imagine the excitement in the villages when Jesus and his entourage appeared. His fame was widespread, and the people were eager to see him and to witness his works. He and his disciples traveled together except on the occasion when Jesus sent them out by teams of two. But there were others with him not often captured by popular imagination. Several women were also his frequent companions. These had been healed of varied diseases and, in gratitude, followed him. Among others, three are named. This is the introduction to Mary Magdalene into the gospel story (Luke 8:1-3). Susanna is not further known, but one fact given regarding Joanna makes it understandable that they "provided for them out of their means." She was the wife of a steward [5] in the household of Herod Antipas, who ruled Galilee. Evidently all three were women of some financial means; and they, at least partially, contributed to the financial support of Jesus and the apostles during their extensive tours.

There was likely a third group in Jesus' company which slowly increased in number as the months passed. From the crowds, most of whom dispersed at close of day or as Jesus moved on, there would inevitably be certain believers who attached themselves to him as disciples and were committed to him. This became a significant band during the two years before the cross, so that the Scriptures state that by the time of his resurrection the believing company in the upper room approximated one hundred and twenty (Acts 1:15). That a number of these had been with Jesus from his early ministry is made plain by the recommendation of Simon Peter. In choosing a replacement for Judas, Peter suggested that they choose "one of the men who have accompanied us during all the time that the Lord Jesus went in and out among us, beginning from the baptism of John" (Acts 1:21-22). Two who met those conditions were Joseph Barsabbas and Matthias, but there were also others.

It is significant as well that one of the postresurrection appearances of Jesus was to some with whom Jesus had made an appointment to meet him on a mountain in Galilee (Matt. 28:16). Apparently speaking of that incident, the Bible declares that "he appeared to more than five hundred brethren at one time" (1 Cor. 15:6). It was to these believers, largely unnamed and unknown, that the Lord delivered his Great Commission, not just to the apostles. The rank and file of kingdom men and women are those whom the King commanded—*go and make disciples!*

---

[5] The steward, Chuza, has been identified by some as the nobleman whose son Jesus healed (John 4:46-53). It is fanciful, but certainly possible.

Galilee was a good locale for finding five hundred. His labors of love there were not unrewarded.

It was not a quiet, isolated event, therefore, when Jesus and his company came to his homeland of Galilee. One should have no difficulty picturing this mission. The caravan, afoot, would move slowly, each one bearing some item of their supplies or equipment. There is no hint that at the earlier stage they lodged or dined with others in their homes. That was done later when the disciples went out in pairs. But now clothing and foodstuffs were carried along with provisions sufficient to last until one of their periodic returns to the base in Capernaum. The chief item of luggage was the large, flat wicker basket, the standard multipurpose vessel of the day. These were the baskets in which the twelve gathered the broken fragments of bread and fish after Jesus fed the five thousand.

If the occasion arose along the way, Jesus would stop to teach or heal, and throngs inevitably gathered from the nearby villages or the well-traveled roads. Otherwise he made his way to the local synagogue, and it was not long until it was noised about that he was in town. It was never a problem to get a crowd. Palestine was astride the main roads from Egypt to Asia Minor, Syria, and Babylonia; and commerce flowed freely in all directions. Tradesmen and spice merchants joined with Romans to hear him. Noblemen and women of rank came also to listen and ask for his help. The merely curious intermingled with the sick, and the adulteress stood alongside the scribe. The Master had chosen his strategy well: multitudes heard him, and he was able to "teach them many things" (Mark 6:33-34). From such diverse elements the men and women of the kingdom were drawn—*if* they had eyes to see!

Another phase of extending the good news was reached when Jesus chose emissaries outside the circle of his apostles. From the wider group of his learners "the Lord appointed seventy others" (Luke 10:1). This was the shape of things to come. He would not always be present in his flesh, and all disciples are also missionaries ("ones sent"). Besides, time was running out; and the harvest made possible by his widespread fame was ripe for gathering. They could cover large areas by teams of two, and he would come along later to investigate their work and meet the needs for which they were inadequate. The essence of their mission was to find those with listening ears; there was no time to reason at length with the hard of heart. Theirs was an announcement meant to be gladly made: "The kingdom of God has come near to you" (Luke 10:8-12).

Luke records that it was a happy mission and that there was a joyful celebration when it had concluded. The occasion of the joy was clearly that as difficult as launching a new kind of kingdom was, still, people responded to its spiritual terms. Preaching was not easy, but it was not hopeless. In spite of the deadening influences of Pharisaic ritual, human hearts still quickened at the truths which perceptive religious leaders had longed for in vain (Luke 10:23-24). When the kingdom came near, some were ready.

THE MYSTERIOUS KINGDOM

It must have been the excitement generated by the preaching that prompted another of the public tests to which Jesus was increasingly subjected. A lawyer of the Pharisees took up with him the subject of how to get the eternal life now so freely talked about. The inquisitor knew the law; and Jesus commended him, telling him what had already been learned—that one must perform *all* the law to be blameless and that to fail at one point was to break the whole law. The man well knew he could not go that route, since it demanded perfection.

Jesus did what he always did in such instances. He dramatized the difference between the definite and the indefinite, the blatant and the subtle. The law spelled out how it should be kept, but love for God with all one's being and love for one's neighbor can never have explicit definition. And the latter way is best!

Things are not less real just because they are indefinable. Indeed, they are likely to be even more valuable—as love is, compared to "things."

As the great teacher illustrated the subject of who is a neighbor, he took occasion to amplify still another aspect unique to his kingdom. The Samaritan of the parable (Luke 10:29-37) had compassion, but no rule to follow. There was no prescribed behavior in the case of a wounded victim of violence. Thus the priest and the Levite, in turn, passed him by. If, however, the rule comes out of the relationship, the one who loves will not look for precepts but will act creatively. So the Samaritan involved himself in the situation, and the circumference of his action needed no prescription. He did what love dictated in that case. It would have been easier to follow a regulation; it was better to follow the heart.

How far should Christians go in dealing with those who, in many fashions, have fallen among thieves? The rule of involvement is the only directive given—identify in love! But are there any limits? One wonders if the original Samaritan would have drawn any. Suppose he had passed that way at other times, and on each occasion had found another who had fallen prey to the brigands. Would he have extended his concern as far as going to the military officials and inquiring as to who was patrolling that road? Would he have gone so far as to take legal action to heal and remedy hurt? The answer somehow seems affirmative.

Jesus always tested Christian behavior by a severe pragmatism—does it work? There was no premium on the piety with which men cried, "Lord, Lord," but on whether they *did* the things which he said. The older brother of the prodigal was not the target of Jesus' parable because he "went away into a far country" but because he would not come in off the porch to the banquet of joy. The builders were not scorned because they built an ugly foundation but because it did not stand when the floods came. The fig tree withered not because its foliage was not adequate but because it produced no figs. The bridesmaids missed the wedding just because having a lamp is no good if it does not work!

The Christian circumference is never static; neither is the Christian's Lord—and that is the reason why the former statement is true. The sons and daughters of the kingdom face each day without code or statute, but they have a relationship with a present friend. Why, then, consult a book of regulations? Instead, ask the friend, "What will you have me to do?" No one ever conceived a religion as vital as that, or as difficult. But that is why it is worth all one's heart and soul and mind and strength—for a lifetime!

The ardor and enthusiasm with which the children of the kingdom are to act is likewise reflected in another vital area where passivity has too often prevailed. Christ threw an entirely new light on prayer. The Old Testament enactments on praying had to do chiefly with public or ritualistic forms, after which things were left in the hands of God. Jesus, as usual, turned the issues inward and made them personal. In Jewish usage, the prayer was in the words—rhetorical, recitative, like chants that must be said. Under his scrutiny, Jesus condemned their use of "vain, empty phrases" and declared that they did not impress God by their "much speaking."

When kingdom citizens invoked the Father, however, they were given a new way of looking at prayer. They have a relational model in which, as in Christian action, the rules are creative and dynamic. There is no evidence that Jesus intended the Model Prayer [6] to become a ritual. It was not an "authorized" prayer. To reduce it to such is to return to the old formulae of prescribed worship. Petitions to the Father are to be constructed from the pattern, but its repetition is not necessarily praying. Blueprints for the contractor are important, but they are not a house to live in; and recipes are useful to the cook, but they are not bread

---

[6] The so-called Lord's Prayer is found in two different forms, but the ideas are harmonious: Luke 11:2-4; Matthew 6:9-13.

to eat. Praying is more than any form of prayer.

THE ENERGETIC KINGDOM

One particular aspect of prayer illuminates the earnestness and zeal which marked his fresh approach to worship and warranted Jesus' use of the word *violence* in regard to kingdom practices. It is his exhortation to boldness and persistence in supplication to God. The Christian has access to God by his identity with Christ, and it is not arrogance to pursue that right. The Father invites the diligent use of the relationship. God is not quickly offended; his goodwill toward his own is not easily bruised. In support of this surprising invitation Jesus employed two of his most energetic parables.

The first was the story of the friend who called at midnight (Luke 11:5-10). For the man to arise and wake his family (likewise asleep in one room) was to ask beyond the call of routine friendship. The need was not that urgent. But the point of the parable is that the man at the door kept knocking; he would not take no for an answer. Jesus used strong words: "importunity" literally means shameless, even impudent! Obviously the Lord did not intend to encourage irreverence, but he did affirm that the people of God do not have to walk on tiptoes before the Almighty as though decorum is the top priority. No, friendship was the reason the night caller exercised his rights to perseverance. He had qualified to act as a friend; and sure enough, his plea was answered, without offense. This is one measure of the privileges of the kingdom.

Even more forceful is the illustration of the unrighteous judge (Luke 18:1-8). Jesus stipulated that he was unjust. He would not render the right verdict, perhaps seeking some advantage in delay. But the woman resorted to an effective tactic; she decided to wear him down. He could scarcely look up from the bench without seeing her in the line of petitioners. She was such a bother to him that in his own mind ("he said to himself") he pictured her as, in effect, assaulting him. The Bible uses one of its most pictur-esque words to describe his view of her tenacity. It is a term literally meaning an "under the eye blow." The unhappy jurist must have wryly smiled as he thought, *She is going to beat me black and blue* [7] *if I do not give her what she wants*. With just such resolution the children of the heavenly realm have access to the King in matters pertaining to the kingdom. They are in business with their Lord, and they are encouraged to be enterpris-ing and unwearied in pressing their claims. Again, the central issue is that there are no boundaries, no terminal points—just involvement and creative relationships!

The meaning of another word of Jesus is best seen against this background. It is the progressive element in the three commands in prayer: "ask . . . seek . . . knock" (Luke 11:9). Apparently the vigilance of knocking stands in contrast with the two preceding verbs. One receives by asking in the first stages of childhood. That is all the infant can do, and parental love does what is best for the child. But in later development more involvement is expected in the process of receiving; there may be a seeking required before finding. At the adult level still more energy is expected, and only then is the "door opened." In prayer, if one asks, "Lord, send justice," will God do it? Probably not—that is, unless the one who prays also knocks on certain doors. God responds to "give me" prayers only when no other activity is necessary. But when the mature stage is reached, the Lord wants perseverance and ardor from his family. Yet once again, here is the "violence" factor in the kingdom of heaven.

THE RICHES OF THE KINGDOM

Jesus Christ has revised the common value systems of every society which he has touched. The Jews of his day never understood him because he overturned their ways of thinking. Even his own

---

[7] This same word is used by Paul in 1 Corinthians 9:27. The Revised Standard Version translates it "pommel."

disciples were astounded at the things he held dear and at those
he was willing to discard. His simply was not traditional mentality.
It was not that he was arbitrary and delighted to upset their
cherished ways. Rather, he acted in this respect just as he had
done in the use of his miraculous powers. He brought the energies
of his higher realm to earth. These were not normal powers for
humans; so also his thoughts were in terms of the coin of the
realm where he lived with the Father. These thoughts were sometimes startling, even to those who wished to learn the secrets
of his kingdom. He looked at earth from the perspective of heaven.

Consequently, he penetrated all the way through money or
"things" to the spiritual use which could be made of them. He
did not scorn the material; he had created it of his own design.
He never thought of the physical realm as being inherently evil,
but he did regard personality as the highest order; and material
things ought to be the tool for the spiritual. So he did not discount
the treasures of others, but looked at the other side first and
measured everything by the moral-spiritual standard. This is what
he called "true riches" (Luke 16:11), and he spoke of those who
had them as being "rich toward God" (Luke 12:21).

His was the same attitude toward position or possessions as
was held by the astronauts preparing to launch to the moon. They
would estimate their possessions and priorities only in regard to
the realm they were about to enter. They did not hesitate to
leave behind automobiles or bank accounts or personal honors
in favor of items and values which pertained to the style of life
in the place where they were going. They would examine everything to determine whether it would serve that end. Logically
their definition of what was desirable would contradict that of
their contemporaries.

These reversed values often caused both Jesus' friends and his
foes to stumble. How could it be possible for a Pharisee to be
bested by a tax collector in the performance of prayers in the
Temple (Luke 18:9-14)? One of them was a representative of

the elite of Israel, unexcelled in devotion to the law and meticulous in the performance of every letter of the statutes. The other was a renegade and self-confessed sinner. Yet the publican, to the consternation of those who heard Jesus' analysis, was the one said to be justified in the sight of God! The pride and vaunted piety of the Pharisee left him poor in spiritual resources as Jesus saw it, while the humbled tax gatherer had tapped the riches of God's grace. That was the assessment of the kingdom view of spiritual need.

Jesus spoke in a similar vein when he affirmed that everyone who receives the gift of God is thereby a steward of that trust. There is a tendency for Christians of small endowment to look longingly at others who seem to have more talent. But when Jesus acted as a spiritual economist, he placed importance on those of lesser gifts: "He who is faithful in very little is faithful also in much" (Luke 16:10; 19:17; Matt. 25:21-23). Every child of the kingdom must settle the issue of his priorities. One cannot be a servant obeying every order of the material world and at the same time give allegiance to the One who is supreme in his regime: "You cannot serve God and mammon" (Luke 16:13). When one sees money as God sees it and holds values as God esteems them, he begins to build reserves of heavenly treasure—true riches indeed. To fail in this spiritual banking obligation is to be a dishonest steward.

God's estimate of worth is supremely portrayed in the best-known parables of Jesus, a cluster of three all based on a unit of one—a lost sheep, a lost coin, a lost son (Luke 15:1-32). In the divine economy, what was valuable stood in sharp contrast to the assessment of the Pharisaic religious leadership of the day. The occasion for the stories was the complaint of these hypocrites that Jesus looked at people and did not see what they saw at all. It was the Master's concern that his way of looking at things should be the standard perspective from the view of his kingdom. So in these parables he superbly illustrated God's priorities in contrast to man's.

In the cases of the sheep and the coin, the traditional view would have been that since so small a percentage was lost, why the fretting over something of small value? There were ninety-nine sheep left; nine coins remained in the treasure box or on the cord (if it were a necklace); and those were good mathematical percentages. The Pharisees might have argued that the law of averages would dictate that there would always be hopeless sinners, so they could be well left alone in favor of those *they* defined as righteous—including themselves.

Not so in Jesus' sight. His heart knew the hopelessness of being lost, and he had come to teach people what they should hold valuable. There was no limit to the lengths he would go to reclaim the lost of his creation, so the factor of energy again enters the picture. The shepherd searches; the woman sweeps—vigilant action was called for, and the restoration of that which was lost was the occasion of joy.

In the instance of the younger son, however, Jesus sketched in a second set of details which gave the narrative almost a three-dimensional look. The central theme was the willful son who acted in folly and lost everything. In sorrow and humility he returned to the expectant father who yearned for him. Joy, then, ought to be unrestrained as it was in the two previous scenes. But no, something is amiss; an ugly note intrudes. Had Jesus concluded the parable with "And they began to be merry" (Luke 15:24), then the trilogy would have in effect been identical, and the Pharisees, to whom the stories were told, might have agreed mildly that compassion was a virtue.

At that point, however, Jesus enlarged the picture so that the Pharisees saw themselves at their unloveliest. The older son, the one who was not an admitted sinner, was seen in his sour and sullen disposition. He assailed his brother and demeaned his father in his own contemptuous pride. Jesus left the ending open. There is no way to know whether the surly "back-porch prodigal" ever went into the house where merriment prevailed. It forever stands as a condemnation to those who deny God's compassion to human sin and error. And it is a graphic portrayal of how the sons and daughters of the kingdom can have in themselves the mind of Christ.

VII
The Things That Have Happened
The Triumph of the King

*"Are you the only visitor to Jerusalem who does
not know the things that have happened there
in these days?"*   *(Luke 24:18)*

Men walk slowly when they are heavy of heart. Thus did the
two men on the Emmaus road that first Sunday afternoon after
the resurrection. They trudged on leaden feet into the sunset,
more preoccupied with the questions they pondered than with
completing their journey. Their demeanor was a reflection of all
the disciples had felt during the two terrible days since their Master
was buried—their hopes were dead. Traveling much of the day,
Cleopas and his companion had not yet covered seven miles.

It is possible the two were father and son, since they appear
to have lived in the same house in the village. They were both
disciples of Jesus and clearly close to the twelve, being aware
of the reported events early that morning. Yet the talk of the
women about seeing angels and the empty tomb seemed to them,
as it did to the apostles, to be "an idle tale" (Luke 24:11). So
perplexed were they over the happenings of the prior three days
that the pair tossed unanswered questions and doubts back and
forth as do men throwing a ball.[1] Their slow pace and intense
gestures must have been obvious to anyone approaching them
from behind—as Jesus himself did!

Not surprisingly, their minds were not properly tuned to recognize him; so they presumed him to be a stranger outbound from
Jerusalem who had overtaken them. They were startled that he
appeared not to know what everyone in the city had been talking
about since the events of Friday—the execution, the earthquake

---

[1] This is the precise force of the verb in Jesus' inquiry of "this conversation
which you are holding with each other" (Luke 24:17).

and unnatural darkness, the curtain before the holy place in the
Temple torn, Romans crying out that surely the Nazarene was
"the Son of God" (Matt. 27:51-54). These things were on everyone's lips. By all human standards it was a perfect setup for a
startling manifestation: a flash of brilliance, a sensational act, an
unearthly spectacle. Instead, with a half-smile Jesus asked, "What
things?" It was such a delightfully normal thing to do.

It was important for the future of the kingdom that the disciples
quickly understand their new relationship with their Lord. He
had always been physically present, but now they had to be
prepared to sense his nearness and to act in fellowship with him
without a visible body. He would come to his own throughout
the ages as the Holy Spirit, and he must be as real to them in
spiritual presence as he had been to his friends in the flesh. The
pattern was, therefore, being set for all the future; and the postresurrection appearances were the necessary transition. What
would an encounter between Christ and Christian be like down
through the years? How would kingdom citizens maintain a vital
nearness to their sovereign? When Jesus communed with his
believers, would the interchange be dramatic or prosaic, supernatural or commonplace?

Christ began to answer those questions from his first experience
with an individual after the stone was rolled away from the
sepulcher. He was not weird or uncanny, not unearthly or fearful.
At first glance Mary Magdalene took him to be a gardener; Cleopas
thought him to be a fellow traveler even after a long conversation;
and the disciples in a boat mistook him for an early-morning
fisherman who was cooking breakfast. He came to his friends
normally, quietly—so naturally that for a while they did not know
who he was. Then they recognized him by characteristic works
and actions—just the way he had been known before.

That is how he still comes—not in a storm of emotional experience, but in the deeper levels of personality. Like the Emmaus
disciples, the eyes of his kingdom men cannot see who is with

them in the way. But then some flash of providence, some burst of light, reveals that they are not unaccompanied in their pilgrimage. At no time since Jesus stepped triumphantly from the grave could it ever be said, "from hence no man has had communion with him." He is life's unseen partner, life's unknown companionship, life's undiscovered guest—always awaiting the instant that dull eyes are opened to recognize him.

There is no clearer commentary on the manner in which the Lord will have fellowship with kingdom men and women than his resumption of normal habits with his followers. One of the distinctive earmarks of his ministry was his conversational skill. Jesus was the master at the art of questioning, his prime teaching tool. It is not strange, then, that his first recorded utterance after being raised was a question to Mary Magdalene: "Why are you weeping?" (John 20:15). Indeed, the writers give only forty-nine verses of actual dialogue by Jesus during his appearances, and thirteen questions are asked within that brief scope. Questioning was then, as it is now, his way of probing deeply into the soul and of stirring the heart to belief, the mind to thought, and the will to action.

A second characteristic act of the Master was eating with those who invited him. There are numerous accounts in the gospel of his participation in suppers, banquets, and feasts. He used food-related events in his parables as well as miraculously providing food on occasions. Conversation at the table had played a major role in his teaching and in the fellowship with his friends. Yet somehow one does not expect eating to be a prominent postresurrection activity, and it may be surprising that three times in his limited appearances he prepared or ate food. (See Luke 24:30,41-43; John 21:6,9-11,15.) It is a significant and beautiful part of the resurrection story that Jesus walked and talked and ate with his own. That is how he was with them in life's normal ways, as undramatic as one friend in dialogue with another—as commonplace as sitting down to a meal with friends. That it was his intent that so it should forever be is made plain by his great summary invitation to every age. He intends to seek out all the individuals of his creation and be aggressive in his appeal—like one knocking at a door. Whoever answers and opens the door will be greeted not by a specter or an apparition, but by a friend who knows how to enter into life's routines: "I will come in to him and eat with him, and he with me" (Rev. 3:20).

The New Covenant

The final chapter of what the two men on the Emmaus road referred to as "the things that have happened" began four days earlier at another table in Jerusalem. Jesus celebrated the Passover meal with his apostles, the last time the twelve were together. There can be no doubt that tensions were increasing. They sensed it in their Master and felt the unmistakable hostility exhibited by the Pharisees, the chief priests, and the scribes. (See Luke 19:39-40; Matt. 21:15-17.) The issue of who Jesus was had been openly precipitated the Sunday before, when he arranged a public entry into Jerusalem and allowed it to turn into a spectacular procession. He did not usually permit himself to be acclaimed, but he knew his time was near. When he faced a showdown with the Jewish authorities, he was determined to confront them as the King-Messiah. So the symbolic ride to the hosannas of the multitudes threw down the gauntlet.

The tumultuous acclamation, however, soon had its inevitable reaction. On Monday he had again driven the hucksters and usurers out of the Temple, making a veiled allusion to the temple of God as being "my house." This further infuriated the priestly establishment, who "sought a way to destroy him" (Mark 11:18). This event was followed by a day of controversy, in which the writers detail the debate which raged between Pharisee and Sadducee and the unaccredited teacher from Nazareth.[2] Every sophis-

---

[2] The frustration of the Jewish leaders is clearly shown in Mark 11:27 to 12:44. Note especially 12:12-13. The debates took place on Tuesday.

ticated device of these experts in the law failed to ensnare him, so on Tuesday evening they resorted to more direct means—they paid Judas Iscariot to betray him.

It is no wonder, then, that the paschal supper on Thursday night found the twelve men in an uncertain mood. It is obvious that whoever should have acted as hosts for the evening had failed to perform the essential duty of bathing the feet of the guests— possibly the two who had been sent to make preparation for the observance (Luke 22:8). The responsibility for that service or some other point of difference caused a sharp contention (Luke 22:24) among the disciples as to which of them should be more important than the others in the kingdom. It was to break this ugly mood that Jesus arose from the table and himself knelt to wash their feet. It was a dark hour for the Master.

Yet Jesus loved these men with whom he had lived and labored since the early days in Galilee and who were about to become the core of the innumerable hosts which would constitute his kingdom. They were immature, frail of faith, prone to err. But they had kept company with their Lord for over two years, and they knew more and believed more than even they realized. Moreover, their commitment to Jesus was about to be tested, and the fire would leave them purified and strengthened—all except one.

Judas had learned more, perhaps, than most of the others. At some point in the past months he had perceived the true nature of the kind of kingdom Jesus was establishing, and it contradicted his expectations. He was not ready to pay the price for that concept of Israel's messianic hopes. His motive for the betrayal of his Master is not made known, but it would seem apparent that profit was not his sole reason. The "thirty pieces of silver" were worth only about twenty dollars. More likely he had been brooding over his unhappy alliance with Jesus, which was sure to involve him in a personally dangerous situation and with no gain to himself. The money, then, would have been an added incentive. That his attitude was negative is seen by John's blunt statement that Judas had turned thief and was stealing from the fund which the disciple band used for living expenses (see John 12:4-6). Moreover, he approached the authorities with his scheme immediately after he had been rebuked by Jesus at a banquet over his reaction toward the use of money. The notion that he acted in pique gains credence in the light of his regret when he realized the enormity of his traitorous deed. At any rate, he showed his true colors and chose favor with the powerful priests rather than casting his lot with a kingdom founded purely on a spiritual base.

A different kind of testing was just ahead for Simon Peter. (Note the accounts in Mark 14:37-42,54,66-72; John 18:10-11.) The refiners' fire was needed to harden the courage of this impetuous spokesman of the disciples before the prophecy of Jesus that Peter should be called "a rock" could be realized. Little did he know that in a matter of weeks he would be standing before thousands in Jerusalem, preaching boldly the death of Christ and pointing the finger of guilt at the Jewish religious rulers who were responsible (see Acts 2:22-24). But when the time came, he would be ready.

The remaining ten men in the upper guest room that night were also to pass the tests. Hammered on the anvil of the years with Jesus, they had slowly been transformed into the character of men who could be foundation stones in the kingdom of heaven and summon others to join themselves in its ranks. They had become new men, fit for a new kind of kingdom. John, once alluded to as a "son of thunder," was made into a son of love (see 1 John 4:7-21). James, his brother, was the first to be faithful to the death (see Acts 12:2). Andrew, quieter than his brother Simon Peter, became an intimate with his Lord (see John 12:20-22). Phillip, who exhibited some dullness (see John 14:8-11), and Nathanael, who once showed skepticism (see John 1:45-50), proved to be solid ministers of Christ. Matthew, the tax collector, wrote a far better record than his assessments; he authored the Gospel which bears his name. The Zealot militant who joined the twelve learned to practice peace. Thomas, the doubter, changed into a convinced witness (John 20:26-29).

THE BLOOD OF THE COVENANT

It was to these intimates that Jesus spoke plainly of a new covenant between God and his people, one not established on the old concept of law and sacrifice. Again, as he so often did, Christ introduced the fact of fulfillment. The old way for God to deal with people stands in sharp contrast with the new. Moses had dramatized vividly the inauguration of the first testament God made with the infant nation of Israel. While the tribes were still camped at Sinai after the exodus, Moses assembled the people before an altar and told them of God's ordinances. "All the words which the Lord has spoken we will do," they cried with unanimous voice (Ex. 24:3-8). As a seal of this agreement Moses took half the blood from the sacrifices, and from basins he threw the blood upon the people, saying, "Behold the blood of the covenant which the Lord has made with you in accordance with all these words." It was by obedience to that covenant that they were saved, and that same principle had already been operative on the night they had escaped the bondage of Egypt.

But obedience to law is not wrong; it is merely inadequate. An excellent preliminary measure, it was not permanent because it could be performed and did not necessarily reach the wellsprings of the human spirit. At the paschal table, Jesus solemnly declared that the wine which symbolized the Passover blood of deliverance would henceforth have a new significance. He lifted the memorial wine and said, "This cup is the new covenant in my blood" (1 Cor. 11:25).

So a new era was about to arrive. The law still reflected the nature and will of Jehovah, but Jesus added another dimension. Not only did he fully show God to men, but he involved the individual in a vital new relationship with himself. The experience is now personal, creative, and life-changing. In short, the old had served its end, and performance was no longer sufficient. The new design was superior and conserved all the values in the former. The kingdom of God would from then on be based on the new agreement with a new sacrifice and a new concept of obedience.

It was not to be a cheaper contract; it was sealed with a far dearer price. Its terms were less rigid, but more rigorous. Kingdom requirements were never to be catalogued but always to be interpreted and applied—in every age of life, at every stage of life, and on every page of life. Indeed, it is far easier to circumcise the body than to live in creative tensions with changing situations. It is simpler to sacrifice a goat than to live up to the sacrifice of Christ. It is much less complex to observe ritual at a temple than to worship "in spirit and in truth." It is less difficult to obey the Ten Commandments than to live intimately with the Commander. This is the Christian's agreement!

A modern age cannot know the feelings of the ancient Hebrew family who watched the choice lamb of the flock being offered at the altar of atonement. When the priest drew the sacrificial knife across the throat and the blood spilled out, there must have been a reaction of awe at the harsh reality that the animal's lifeblood purchased the forgiveness of their sins. Similarly, any person who looks on the cross must stand amazed and even fearful at the reality and consequences of sin. The Lamb of God offered himself as a sacrifice. It was God's new way to make once for all a far better offering for sin, one that need not be repeated—except in human experience. He died because he came to identify with all mankind and bear their guilt; and, since the disease of the sinful rebel will is as deep as life's blood itself, so must be the cure. As it was essential for him to die for every man's sins, so must every man die for them too—by identity in faith with Christ who paid the price. That leaves the redeemed individual *involved*, and when one accepts his redemption he also accepts his kingdom!

There is, thereby, a vital aspect of the cross experience of Jesus usually lost or hidden amid the emotions stirred by his death. It is that his kingship is highlighted more intensely at the crucifixion events than at any other point of his life. No less than eleven times in the brief hours of his trial and being placed on the cross there are allusions to him as King and to his kingdom.

The pattern was set in the first hearing before Pilate the Roman governor. An accusation was made: "We found this man . . . saying that he himself is Christ a king" (Luke 23:2-3). When asked to reply, Jesus confirmed it, but asserted that his kingdom was "not of this world" (John 18:33-37). The soldiers no doubt heard the discussion, and when next they handled Jesus they mocked him by fashioning a crown for his head, which they made from a thorn tree. Finding an old purple toga in the barracks, they draped it over his shoulders and made sport of him, jeering, "Hail, King of the Jews!" (See John 19:2-3; Mark 15:16-19.) Thus arrayed, he was then brought out of the palace to the mob; and Pilate taunted the people by saying, "Then what shall I do with the man whom you call the King of the Jews?" (Mark 15:12). This was a deliberate insult by the governor, who hated the Jews; and after a while he repeated it, adding "Shall I crucify your King?" (See John 19:14-15.)

The most significant use of regal language was inadvertent. Pilate did not intend to state one of the supreme truths of history. His motive was a final gesture of ridicule at the Jewish authorities. Yet all four Gospel writers see it as highly symbolic and tell how the Christ died—under a sign written in three languages for all the world to see: "Jesus of Nazareth, the King of the Jews" (John 19:19-22).[3] It was a king who died on the cross, and he rules supreme over his kingdom!

HE IS NOT HERE: BEHOLD THE PLACE

It ought not to be surprising that discipleship should begin at

---

[3] Note further references to the kingship issue in Mark 15:32 and Luke 23:42.

the cross. For some it did. Even in the atmosphere of fear and
suspicion created by the Sanhedrin, two men of their number
boldly took a stand. A man from the village of Arimathea named
Joseph, although a counselor, had been a secret disciple. Under
the compulsion of Jesus' death he was moved to declare himself,
and at considerable risk he asked to bury the Lord's body. It
is noteworthy that Luke says of him, "he was looking for the
kingdom of God" (Luke 23:51). Joining him was another member
of the ruling council who had appeared before in the Gospel
story—Nicodemus. Already this influential man had spoken up
in open session but was not at that time an avowed follower
of Jesus. Now he also emerged from the safety of secrecy and
joined Joseph in the ritual of burial.[4]

It will probably never be given to mankind to know the manner
of the resurrection, yet his mind will forever be intrigued by this
climactic event of redemptive history. Speculation is inevitable
and may be fruitful, but it is likely more useful to view the evidence
as certain of the disciples did on that first day of the week. It
seems clear that what they saw was the occasion of their belief
that Jesus was alive even before they saw him in person. The
sight also suggested how it might have happened.

The issue goes back to the burial in keeping with Jewish custom.
Preparation consisted of wrapping the body in linen cloths and
of folding in spices. Mark, who possibly got his details from Peter,
an eyewitness, took care to use a verb which means "to wind"
or "to roll in" when he described the process of enshrouding
(see Mark 15:46). John adds a further detail: a napkin had covered
the head, separate from the winding-sheets. On first alarm that
the Lord's body was not in the tomb, John and Simon Peter ran
to the garden and into the sepulcher knowing what they could
expect. If the body were there, then it should be wrapped as
Joseph and Nicodemus had left it and had sealed the tomb with
the great stone rolled in place. If robbers had rifled the grave,

---

[4] John alone tells the Nicodemus story. See John 7:45-52; 19:39-41.

the clothing would be disarranged. If the body were stolen away, then there would be no trace of clothes or spices. At the moment they could foresee no other alternatives.[5]

What they saw shook them both. First Peter, then John, stood speechless as their eyes absorbed every feature on the stone shelf where Jesus' body had lain. They could distinguish the form of the folds where the limbs and torso had been wrapped; but the clothes, now empty, were lying undisturbed. Even the head covering was by itself in its proper place. It did not take long for the two to realize what they were seeing. He had not been taken away; he had not struggled free; it was as though he had calmly and majestically passed in spirit form through the grave clothes and, contemptuous of death, had left them there!

They would not have understood as much as modern man any notion of spiritual metamorphosis. It would have been beyond their comprehension how ice, under proper temperature, could turn into steam, escape to another vessel, and, lowering the temperature, become ice again. But they knew their Lord and had grown accustomed to seeing him act on a spiritual plane above their expectations. The evidence was compelling; and John, who told the story, could reach only one conclusion: "He saw and believed." Whatever had happened, Jesus himself had done it! They did not then fully understand the resurrection, but that night Jesus would visit them when the entire believing band was assembled and chide them at finding faith so difficult. He would at that time prove that the same Jesus whom they had seen entombed now stood before them. "See my hands and my feet," he said, "that it is I myself; handle me, and see; for a spirit has not flesh and bones as you see that I have" (Luke 24:39).

It was a difficult lesson, but they learned it well. In a period of six weeks they saw him many times; and although he did not resume the same routines as before, he was still their Master, and he spoke with them in great detail of what he expected of

[5] The episode is described in detail in John 20:3-10.

them as they launched his kingdom. So convinced were they that he was alive and with them that they acted after the resurrection just as they had before his death. In the record of the early church in the book of Acts, his friends preached and taught about him as though he had not gone away at all. Indeed, he had not.

It is essential to the kingdom of heaven that such a pattern continue. He still comes to his friends, interprets himself, and declares, "You are witnesses of these things" (Luke 24:48). Each member of his realm, without exception, is under commission to bear witness of what he knows to those outside. There is no alternate plan! No more than a Christian can pay a priest to secure his salvation can he employ a minister to discharge his obligation to be an evangelist—a bearer of good news.

Yet, in its truest sense, the gospel can never be fully told by words, because it came in a person. So only personal characteristics are sufficient for the communication of the news of the kingdom. As the Lord always identified himself in terms of his deeds, so must his disciples have the character which grants them the right to speak. A witness is not one who tells what he knows; rather, he is one who knows something to tell; he is possessor of a fund of experience. If, then, the character is beyond reproach, he may be allowed to testify.

It is said of Francis of Assisi that on an occasion he invited one of his followers to go with him into the villages and preach. As they passed through the gates they saw the children, and Francis blessed them. He counseled with the parents; he touched the hurt; he spoke comfort to the poor and suffering. Before they realized it, the two men had traversed the town and into the open country. "I thought we were going into the village to preach," said the young man. Responded the kindly Francis, "There is no use going anywhere to preach unless you preach everywhere you go."

The greatest of Masters made it his last word: "All authority in heaven and on earth has been given to me. Go therefore and make disciples of all nations" (Matt. 28:18-19). Every citizen of the kingdom is under those orders until the King returns.